EX LIBRIS

BIBLIOSTYLE

BIBLIO·STYLE

HOW WE LIVE AT HOME WITH BOOKS

NINA FREUDENBERGER

WITH SADIE STEIN

PHOTOGRAPHS BY

SHADE DEGGES

CLARKSON POTTER/PUBLISHERS

NEW YORK

Published in the United States
by Clarkson Potter/Publishers,
an imprint of Random House,
a division of Penguin Random
House LLC, New York.
clarksonpotter.com

CLARKSON POTTER is a trademark
and POTTER with colophon is a registered
trademark of Penguin Random House LLC.

Library of Congress Cataloging-
in-Publication Data has been
applied for.

ISBN 978-0-525-57544-3
Ebook ISBN 978-0-525-57545-0

Printed in China
Interior and cover design by Mia Johnson

10 9 8 7 6 5 4 3

First Edition

P. 1 A quiet corner in writer Jonathan Safran-Foer's Brooklyn home.

PREVIOUS Books are stacked on the pianos in James Fenton's and Darryl Pinckney's Harlem brownstone.

FOLLOWING Photographer Todd Hido's San Francisco home's book room.

FOR JULIAN,
WOLF & MIKE

CONTENTS

INTRODUCTION

I HAVE ALWAYS BEEN most interested in the question of what makes a house a home. What are the elements that move a house beyond its physical structure and provide the warmth that we all crave? In my fifteen years as a designer, I've come to understand that the answer is simple: It is about surrounding ourselves with things we love.

While exploring homes around the world for my first book, *Surf Shack*, I came to the conclusion that if you start with your passions, beauty will follow. And in this case, the beauty comes from the owners' love of books.

Books are beautiful objects in their own right—their bindings and covers—and the space they fill on shelves or stacked on coffee tables in colorful piles add balance and texture to any room. And just like any other part of a home, books require maintenance: They need to be dusted, categorized, rearranged, and maintained. Our relationship with them is dynamic and ever changing.

But our connection to them goes beyond the material. In each house we visited, the libraries were the heart of the home, meaningful to the collectors' lives. In this book, we tried to capture what they brought to the home—the life and spirit books added. Some subjects have working libraries they constantly reference; others fill their shelves with the potential pleasures of the unread. When we visited the homes, many people could find favorite books almost by osmosis, using systems known only to themselves.

In choosing our subjects, we were not merely interested in the beautiful and perfectly curated rooms, the most extensive collections, or those shelves filled only with rare first editions—although there's plenty of beauty on display. This book is not about unattainable libraries, any more than it is about perfectly decorated homes. Rather, it's about the power of books to tell stories, in both the literal and figurative sense. As we found repeatedly, surrounding yourself with books you love tells the story of your life, your interests, your passions, your values. Your past and your future. Books allow us to escape, and our personal libraries allow us to invent the story of ourselves—and the legacy that we will leave behind.

There's a famous quote attributed to Cicero: "A room without books is like a body without a soul." If I suspected this before, I know it now. I hope you'll find as much pleasure in discovering these worlds as we did.

the *the* SENTIMENTALISTS

A HOUSE OF
A THOUSAND STORIES

ATHENA MCALPINE
Puglia, Italy

STRIDING DOWN THE VENERABLE STONE HALLS of Il Convento di Santa Maria di Costantinopoli with her white wolfhound, Gloria, following at her heels like a benevolent familiar, Athena McAlpine can identify the spine of every book almost without looking. And there are thousands. "These are all on India. That's interiors, of course, and here's photography. This shelf is entirely chick lit—pool literature—for the guests." The stacks are sorted by subject; the books that line the locked shelves are alphabetized by author.

The Greek-born, London-bred McAlpine and her husband, Alastair, lived in the Convento together before his death four years ago, and she is quick to say that any discussion of the couple's massive library of first editions is, necessarily, a discussion of both of them. It was he who attempted to acquire first editions of all the books they loved—and clearly they loved many. Even the Jackie Collins are first editions.

The Convento is a former Franciscan monastery and onetime tobacco factory, which now functions both as McAlpine's home and as a discreet hotel. Set in a barren, wildly beautiful stretch of the Puglian countryside, the rambling property is both stunning and comfortable. While the barrel-vaulted ceilings, the cloisters, and the library, which seems to run for miles, all evoke the past, this is no museum: filled with modern art, mementos of her various homelands, succulent gardens, and books on every conceivable subject, it's a dynamic and idiosyncratic place that wears its age and its beauty easily.

Like the rest of the property, the bookshelves are a mixture of private and public, *some* open to guests and others locked away for private use. Although she still receives regular shipments of books from London's independent bookstore John Sandoe Books ("It's like Christmas when they arrive"), McAlpine is about to undertake a

OPPOSITE "Pool reads" for hotel guests to enjoy.

PREVIOUS PAGES The cabinets are filled with first editions, and the books are stacked along the hall by subject.

LEFT A rotating selection of photography and art books in one of the Convento's common spaces.

ABOVE Textiles and materials found during recent travels.

ABOVE LEFT The building dates back to the seventeenth century.

ABOVE RIGHT African sculpture at a turn in the stair.

BELOW A book from Marlene Dietrich's personal library.

OPPOSITE A book-filled guestroom.

major winnowing of the library. "I just feel like a lightening, or a purge, is somewhat imminent. I'm not a purger, but I feel I need to purge. In a way, I'm very happy for my husband because he didn't have to deal with any of it, he wasn't ill, he was enjoying his environment right to the end, and I think actually that's a great luxury. But everything about this place is totally caught up with my marriage and my husband and what we created together, and it's very difficult to move forward when you've got quite this much past. Even from a practical point of view, I'd like to have the space to let some more books into my life."

There are many books, however, that are sacrosanct: the first edition *Huck Finn,* for instance, that was a Christmas gift from her husband. McAlpine is particularly interested in collecting books that were the basis for film adaptations she also loves—*The Big Sleep, Night of the Hunter, The African Queen, To Have and Have Not, Looking for Mr. Goodbar,* to name just a few.

And then there's what might be called the VIP cabinet, which contains "all books that have a special meaning for me, or a story. Books I don't want to get misplaced." However, it's a system that would be inscrutable to the casual observer: Some were written by friends. One novel, *Sea of Love,* is set in the Convento. There is one shelf devoted only to dog books; another to especially beautiful editions. There are the books she read at the height of her grief. Oddities like J. Edgar Hoover's *Masters of Deceit,* signed to actor Adolphe Menjou, bearing Marlene Dietrich's bookplate, keep company with both erotica and an especially pretty copy of *Diary of a Provincial Lady.*

Such eclecticism reflects the breadth of McAlpine's interests and curiosity. Currently, she is on a Graham Greene kick, and a discussion of *Travels with My Aunt* gives way to a debate about Shakespeare's possible subversive Catholicism. She loves to give away copies of favorite books,

like the cantankerous art critic Brian Sewell's paean to dogs, and is irrepressible in her enthusiasms, anecdotes ("he was deeply, deeply, deeply, *deeply* eccentric"), and quotations. McAlpine went to drama school; she does a very good Diana Vreeland impression and knows much of *The Duchess of Malfi* by heart.

And "just because I have a horrible feeling I will die without having read any Proust, I have to keep this one," she says, indicating a beautiful edition of *Remembrance of Things Past*. She replaces it carefully in the special cupboard so she'll know exactly where it is.

"I'D LIKE TO HAVE THE SPACE TO LET MORE BOOKS INTO MY LIFE."

ABOVE LEFT The Convento is filled with surprise reading nooks.

ABOVE RIGHT Athena McAlpine

OPPOSITE Interiors and film books, stacked by size.

ABOVE RIGHT A path along the cloister.

OPPOSITE A cupboard holds textiles from around the world.

A READER'S PILGRIMAGE

EVEN IN A CITY AS BOOKSHOP-RICH AS LONDON, Persephone is something very special: a shop dedicated solely to selling the Persephone imprint, which, in turn, is dedicated to reprints of primarily female-authored, twentieth-century neglected texts. The gray-blue-jacketed books, with their distinctive patterned endpapers, fill most of Nicola Beauman's cozy Bloomsbury shop, where customers—almost cultlike in their devotion—can buy all 130 Persephone editions, perhaps enjoy an apple from the local farm share, and revel in the space's serenity.

ABOVE A reader's pilgrimage stop in Bloomsbury.

OPPOSITE A vintage dress displayed alongside Persephone editions.

WHERE EVERY CHAIR
IS THE READING CHAIR

KATHLEEN HACKETT & STEPHEN ANTONSON
Brooklyn, New York

"HE DOESN'T LIKE IT when I call them his *obsession*," says the writer Kathleen Hackett of her husband, Stephen Antonson, indicating the mountains of books in the living room of their Carroll Gardens brownstone.

"My *interest*," corrects Antonson, an artist who's developed a cult following for his plaster of paris fixtures, furniture, and sculpture.

"Let's say it's on the spectrum," says Hackett, whose own library—she's a cookbook author—comingles with art and design books throughout the house.

Certainly, books are everywhere: In the gracious front room, which retains the details of the Victorian parlor it was, piles of art and design books fill the tables, surround the fireplace, are stacked on every surface. And that's to say nothing of the bookshelves Antonson built throughout the house. (Their sons' bunk bed even includes a Donald Judd–inspired built-in bookshelf filled with Hardy Boys.) While the space is, naturally, filled with the chalky creations for which Antonson is known, books provide splashes of color and energy everywhere.

"Including the toilet," adds Antonson.

"You had to go there," says Hackett.

The art and design books, of course, function as reference for Antonson and his studio assistants. "I'll sit in the living room and I'll go through them, either looking for something I remember seeing, or for something to catch my eye and inspire me. And with books, there's still an element of serendipity; you see new elements from day to day."

"With the Internet, it's like a road map," says Hackett. "You know exactly what you're looking for and you go there. Whereas with books—and this is true of cookbooks, too—they're alive."

> "IN EVERY SINGLE SEAT IN THIS HOUSE, YOU CAN PICK UP A BOOK."

OPPOSITE Books obscure a controversial TV.

25

The library contains the classics of design—Poire, Rand, Giacometti, Jean-Michel Frank—as well as Julia Child and Richard Olney. But there are often new acquisitions, depending on the project at hand. At the moment, Hackett is coauthoring a book on bread (there is sourdough starter burbling on the marble kitchen counter), so an entire shelf—next to a highly coveted reading spot known as "The Chair"—has been given over to bread tomes.

A trip to the Strand is always liable to result in five new books. "Part of what's great there," says Antonson, "is that they have exhibition and auction catalogs that often have pieces—prototypes or casts—that you'll never see in other books, let alone on the Internet. And then they'll throw in a free tote bag if you spend a hundred dollars . . . if the Strand ever went away, it'd send me into a spiral."

So, how do they keep on top of it? "A lot of it is in the basement," says Hackett, and the stone-floored cellar is indeed lined with book-filled Metro shelves. "The general rule in this house," says Antonson, "is that no book ever gets thrown away. Ever." And so there are periodic donations: to used bookstores, thrift stores, and friends.

Books also move regularly between the house and Antonson's Gowanus studio. "It's a dynamic situation," as he characterizes it, and indeed, the studio contains several laden bookshelves.

Recently, the family has acquired its first TV, a controversial purchase, which now lives inside the fireplace—but is surrounded, and often covered, by art books. "It's like snow," says Hackett. "We dig it out from the books."

ABOVE Stacks of inspiration in Antonson's Gowanus studio.

BELOW You have to move books from every surface, says the couple.

OPPOSITE The Chair—the most coveted reading spot in the house.

ABOVE Kathleen Hackett and Stephen Antonson at home.

OPPOSITE, ABOVE Both Antonson and Hackett tend
to have a few books going at once.

OPPOSITE, BELOW A bureau-bookshelf in the couple's bedroom.

"THE GENERAL RULE
IN THIS HOUSE
IS THAT NO BOOK
EVER GETS THROWN
AWAY. EVER."

BOOKS, BOOKS
EVERYWHERE!

KARL OVE KNAUSGAARD

Malmö, Sweden

KARL OVE KNAUSGAARD CAN REMEMBER the first book he ever loved. "It was a children's picture book called *Karius,*" he recalls. "Very popular in Norway. About a little girl and her garden; I can still see the pictures."

It's a far cry from Knausgaard's own work, the introspective, best-selling multi-volume autobiography *My Struggle*. But then, as he says, "We all must begin somewhere."

Knausgaard lives part-time in Sweden, not far from the Danish border. The house he shares with his family is a Scandinavian idyll, ordered and picturesque, set in a small orchard. His office, however, is another realm. The wood-frame outbuilding is, to the casual observer, complete chaos: rooms of overflowing ashtrays and dirty dishes, piles of loose notes, and stack upon stack of books. His numerous awards are displayed casually in the bathroom; on the screen of an aged desktop computer, the cursor blinks midsentence on what looks like a perilously unsaved document.

Knausgaard alternates between periods of intense reading and not reading at all; the mountains of books are, he says, largely aspirational. He classifies them into three categories: books he wants to read, books he has to read, and books he feels he ought to read. In the last, unchanging category—which he calls the superego heap—you'll find a large number of books on philosophy.

His bookshelves are equally varied; along with international editions of his own books are Turgenev, Anne Carson, Maggie Nelson, Kazuo Ishiguro, and scores of contemporary Norwegian novelists. Although you'll find Nordic crime novels, he says he usually

> "I THINK THE WAY PEOPLE TREAT BOOKS IS A BIT OF AN INDICATOR OF THEIR CHARACTER."

OPPOSITE The study where Knausgaard does most of his writing.

only reads them when he's depressed. "I have a bad memory and too many books," distributed among four homes, "so I waste lots of time walking around searching" for a specific book. This has its upside: he's often surprised by books he'd forgotten. "I'm convinced everything can be useful for my writing, so I buy a lot of books randomly, about subjects I think one day can make it into a novel."

He reads before bed, and while traveling—albeit reluctantly. "I hear a voice that says reading is lazy," so accordingly, he only reads in the evening—when, he says, he's too tired to remember what he read the night before.

On the seeming chaos, he is philosophical. "I think the way people treat books is a bit of an indicator of their character," he says. "And in many ways, I'm a very careless person."

ABOVE LEFT The family's converted farmhouse in Malmö, Sweden.

ABOVE RIGHT Karl Ove Knausgaard.

OPPOSITE, ABOVE LEFT The office is housed in an outbuilding on the property.

OPPOSITE, ABOVE RIGHT The floor, Knausgaard's office.

OPPOSITE, BELOW How the literary sausage gets made.

OVERLEAF By his own admission, Knausgaard can't find his books.

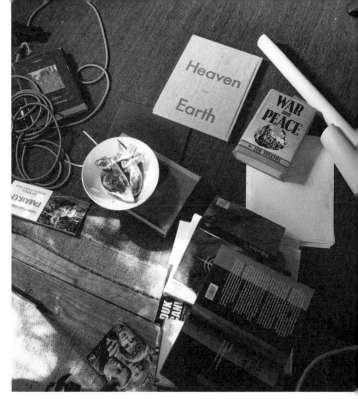

"I'M CONVINCED EVERYTHING
CAN BE USEFUL FOR MY
WRITING, SO I BUY A LOT
OF BOOKS RANDOMLY, ABOUT
SUBJECTS I THINK ONE DAY
CAN MAKE IT INTO A NOVEL."

PEAK INTEREST

THE LIBRARIES OF PRIVATE CLUBS ARE FASCINATING in their monomania, whether it be the American Society for Psychical Research's library in New York, the collection of occult works at Los Angeles's Magic Castle, or the Mechanics' Institute Library in San Francisco. The Alpine Club, located in the Shoreditch neighborhood of London, is a good example. The oldest Alpine explorers' club in the world (the term applies to the style of climbing as well as the region), the library contains thousands of books on the history, flora, fauna, biography, and fictional representations of alpine climbing. In addition, visitors may peruse early maps of the Alps, read the journals of famous explorers—some retrieved from climbers who didn't make it—club records dating back to the nineteenth century, the published journals of various climbing clubs around the world, Edmund Hillary's membership application, and the odd pair of donated 1920s boots or Victorian crampons. To join this one, a member must have climbed "twenty respectable routes in the Alps or other regions." Asked if he was a climber himself, librarian Nigel Buckley replied, "They wouldn't let me through the door otherwise."

OPPOSITE Journals, atlases, history, poetry, fiction: If it's to do with alpine climbing, chances are you'll find it in the library.

A READING ROOM
OF ONE'S OWN

R. O. BLECHMAN & MOISHA KUBINYI
Hudson Valley, New York

"It was *Mrs. Dalloway*," says R. O. Blechman, surveying the shelf of books dedicated to members of the Bloomsbury Group in his living room. "That's what started it all. I picked up a copy at a downtown bookstore, and I just thought—*wow*. It moved me like nothing I'd ever read."

By his own account, Blechman—a legendary illustrator, animator, and cartoonist—"although I hate that word, *cartoonist*"—has many passions, and many collections; the nineteenth-century farmhouse he shares with his wife, Moisha Kubinyi, in Columbia County, New York, is testament to it. But Bloomsburiana, as the field is known, is among his most beloved. The shelves of books by Virginia and Leonard Woolf, Lytton Strachey, Maynard Keynes, Bertrand Russell, and assorted Hogarth Press authors hold pride of place in a built-in bookcase near a generous fireplace. Like the rest of the house, it's both airy and cozy, a mixture of antiques and art and jewel-like colors that harmonizes naturally with the house's original layout and low ceilings. Kubinyi, who worked for many years as a clothing designer, supervised the interiors as well as the rolling grounds; "she has an amazing eye," says her husband.

While it was the prose that first attracted Blechman, he quickly became enchanted with the iconic look of the Hogarth Press books, many of which were designed by Virginia Woolf's sister, Vanessa Bell. Indeed, some of his most prized books are not, in fact, his favorite novels: "I've always drowned a bit in *The Waves*," he admits. "But then, Vanessa Bell didn't read them all, either!"

Although the collection started with Woolf, and that first copy of *Mrs. Dalloway* holds a special place in his heart, over the years Blechman has become particularly attached to the figure of Leonard Woolf, Virginia's husband, publisher, cheerleader, sometime-caregiver, and full-time devotee. He once wrote an entire illustrated story

OPPOSITE A window seat reading nook in Blechman's
Hudson Valley farmhouse.

"EVERYTHING
HE READS IS,
ACCORDING TO
HIM, THE BEST
BOOK EVER."

ABOVE LEFT R. O. Blechman in his studio.

LEFT The house is filled with several generations'
worth of books.

ABOVE RIGHT A corner of the living room.
Blechman credits the eye of his wife, Moisha
Kubinyi, for all decorative decisions.

OPPOSITE The house looks out on an ever-
changing Hudson Valley landscape.

about Leonard for the *New York Times*. "He was one of the most remarkable, selfless figures in the history of literature, I think," says Blechman, over tea in the sunny dining room. "I don't own very much of his"—in the original, that is—"but I love him." Over the years, the collection has come to contain a huge number of historical and reference works, biographies, and books from the private libraries of several members of the circle, including Lady Ottoline Morrell—who annotated a book of Thomas Hardy poems with spidery check marks and *x*'s, depending on her preferences—and Vita Sackville-West.

While the bulk of the Bloomsburiana is kept in the sitting room, the house overflows with books: Fiction and essays jostle one another in a library filled with antique stained glass and cushioned window seats; upstairs, their grown sons' rooms now function as de facto studies. There are full sets of vintage, red-bound Harper's histories, essays by William Morris and Max Nordau, countless biographies, and the youthful libraries of their sons. "I'll bet you've never been to a house that contains fifteen books by Prince Kropotkin!" says Moisha, referring to one's anarchist phase. "I picked one up the other day; extremely interesting!"

Almost every room feels right for reading and is filled with armchairs and lamps, but weather permitting, the couple says they especially like to read outdoors, overlooking the pond where they swim and the bird feeders they tend to. "We read very different things," says Moisha. These days, she reads a great deal about the environment; her husband loves essays.

The house is filled not only with books, but also with art—oil landscapes and woodcuts, portraits and drawings—much of it by Moisha's parents, artists Doris Hall and Kalman Kubinyi.

Blechman's own work is housed in a large outbuilding a few steps from the main house, which contains a serene, light-filled studio, a room devoted to shelved archives of his art and late magazine, *Story*, a shower, and a small kitchen. (It can function as a guesthouse as needed.)

In the eaved bedroom the couple shares, the low bed—overlooking the fields and woods—is surrounded by neat piles of books. Every night, before going to sleep, Moisha reads from Thoreau. Her husband's tastes are more catholic; at the moment, he's loving the work of Stefan Zweig. "Everything he reads is, according to him, the best book ever," remarks Moisha. "But this is really incredible!" he says. "I really lucked out!"

ABOVE LEFT "We have a little bit of everything," says Blechman.

ABOVE RIGHT The couple maintained the house's original layout.

BELOW The living room and library; the shelf on the right is filled with Bloomsburiana.

OPPOSITE A mix of fiction and nonfiction in the study.

OVERLEAF The house is filled with art, much of it by the family.

A CABINET
OF WONDERS

PIERRE LE-TAN*
Paris, France

"I DON'T CALL MYSELF A BIBLIOPHILE," says the illustrator Pierre Le-Tan, gesturing to the twelve-foot-high bookshelves that line the salon of his Left Bank apartment. "Those people like original editions with certain paper or watermarks. . . . That doesn't interest me at all. Bibliophiles prefer the pages uncut, some of them; the edition might be wonderful, but what is the point of a book you can't read? I just like to read my books." Le-Tan is, by his own admission, a lover of beautiful things—but it's obvious he lives *with* his hundreds of volumes rather than *among* them.

To see a Pierre Le-Tan drawing is to recognize it at once: His fifty years' worth of illustrated books, *New Yorker* covers, ad campaigns, collaborations, and portraits are characterized not just by a distinctive crosshatch aesthetic but also by a sort of spare solitude. He creates a remarkably intricate world and yet somehow distills it to its essence: It requires attention.

This same tension—between restraint and maximalism, and seriousness and whimsy, and curatorial pride and irreverence—is immediately visible on Le-Tan's bookshelves, too. Eighteenth-century almanacs keep company with Allen Ginsberg, who sits next to novels in German and Spanish. The intricately figured Prousts are from the library of Peggy Guggenheim; Le-Tan says he plans to read from these exact editions when he rereads the series.

Le-Tan claims the airy apartment was spare when he moved in; he also claims to miss the serenity. He is, he admits, a hoarder; if he sees something interesting he acquires it. "It's really terrible." He sighs. But the vivid beauty of the current space, where acid-green walls play host to sixteenth-century marble busts, Warhol drawings, antique textiles in glowing jewel tones, masks, Hokusai prints, Hockneys, and, of course, shelf after shelf of books—is remarkably warm and inspiring. One has only to

OPPOSITE Any semblance of organization in his Paris library
"is an illusion," says Pierre Le-Tan.

This interview was conducted with Pierre Le-Tan not long before we received the sad news of his passing.

look to see beauty; to look again is to find a secret, a joke, or another tiny world hidden within this one. Consider a beautifully bound eighteenth-century volume the dapper Le-Tan plucks unerringly from a shelf of miniature books: He has filled the blank vellum pages with his own tiny handwriting and delicate drawings, a sly homage. Nearby, in front of a large shelf of Cecil Beaton first editions, is a collection of exquisitely wrought netsuke and a Giacometti sketch; among their ranks is a tiny plastic Donald Trump troll doll. At one point, his three-year-old daughter, Zoë, saunters in and makes herself comfortable, clearly at ease amid the treasures.

While his interests span art, Turkish rugs, and all manner of *objets,* Le-Tan says books have always held a special place in his home, and have from the time he was a child. While other children played games, the young Le-Tan "made fake books"—a practice he's refined in the ensuing years. It was his father, the celebrated Vietnamese painter Lê Phô', who inspired his vast collection of books on Asian art. (Somehow it does not seem surprising that designer Olympia Le-Tan, his daughter, should have created a cult line of whimsical minaudière clutches inspired by beautiful book covers.)

Portions of the library are given over to works that have informed his more than thirty books, which he says are the ones closest to his heart. There are also shelves of classical poetry, oxblood-bound poetry, and art history. "I'm interested in all kinds of arts—Asian, European, Islamic antiquities," he says. "So the influences

ABOVE LEFT Le-Tan is always on the lookout for fresh pine twigs to scent the entryway.

ABOVE RIGHT Le-Tan prefers "hoarder" to "collector," but the results are layered and beautiful.

OPPOSITE A mix of comfort and style: This sofa is where Le-Tan reads.

ABOVE Medieval vellum, textiles, and miniatures: Each corner tells a story.

OPPOSITE To Le-Tan, even the most unembellished books have beauty.

"MY DREAM WOULD
BE TO HAVE THEM
ALL IN CATEGORIES,
ORGANIZED. I ALWAYS
SAY I'M GOING TO
MAKE A PROPER LIST
OF AT LEAST THE
MOST PRECIOUS BOOKS.
I KNOW IF I WENT
THROUGH THEM
ALL, I'D FIND BOOKS
I'D COMPLETELY
FORGOTTEN."

are all sorts of influences. I can't say such and such artist was an enormous influence on me; it's little things in different artists that influenced me. What you do, of course, is a result of looking at all these things." He takes his initial inspiration from a line in a book, an image, an object, and never knows where it might be found.

The shelves of Japanese art volumes look well organized, but "it's an illusion," he says sadly. "Nothing is organized here." In addition to the books that fill the shelves and make haphazard piles on the floor, there are several hundred boxes of books in storage. "My dream would be to have them all in categories, organized. I always say I'm going to make a proper list of at least the most precious books. I know if I went through them all, I'd find books I'd completely forgotten. But when I do see them, I find I know every book—where I've bought it, who had given it to me, when and where I read it. It's wonderful, but if I start, it's endless." Indeed, when asked about the particularly beautiful marbled spine of a volume across the room, he can identify it at once: the poetry of Louise de Vilmorin, bought at a nearby bookseller some fifteen years prior.

Le-Tan has set no routine—at times, he might work all day and at others spend weeks waiting for inspiration. Or, for that matter, reading. "I've got no discipline for anything," he says. A homebody, he works—and reads—on an overstuffed, somewhat sagging lilac sofa clearly chosen for comfort, surrounded by stacks of new books in French and English. To the casual observer, the piles of new, unadorned Gallimard editions might look uninspiring. But, says Le-Tan, "quite ordinary books are beautiful."

ABOVE Each tableau makes you look, then look again.

OPPOSITE, ABOVE Despite their number—and sometimes casual display—
Le-Tan can identify all his books from a glance at their bindings.

OPPOSITE, BELOW Pierre Le-Tan with his daughter Zoë.

RARE BIRDS

"I describe us as a *ruly* elephant," says Ed Maggs of his sprawling family business. Since its founding in 1853—and through a recent move to a new Bloomsbury headquarters—Maggs Bros. has prospered as one of the world's most important antiquarian booksellers and is a decided London institution. Featuring a diverse catalog that ranges from illuminated manuscripts to first editions of Joyce, Maggs has managed to maintain relationships with some clients literally for centuries, while introducing a new generation to the pleasures of bibliomania, and what Maggs terms a welcome and reinvigorated "quest for the authentic." While the walls may feature generations of former Maggses, the staff is filled with "wonderful young booksellers." As to the firm's unwavering commitment to the printed object, Maggs explains his reason simply: "Nothing but the fact that these things *matter*."

ABOVE The business was founded by Uriah Maggs in 1853
and is still family owned.

OPPOSITE Rare books in Maggs's Bloomsbury headquarters.

the *the* INTUITIVES

WHERE STYLE
MEETS SUBSTANCE

EMMANUEL DE BAYSER
Berlin, Germany

"I DON'T WANT TO SOUND PRETENTIOUS," says Emmanuel de Bayser, "but I don't understand people who don't have books."

A noted collector and a proprietor of concept stores in Paris and Berlin, de Bayser is known for his discerning eye and a sleekly unified aesthetic. In his Gendarmenmarkt apartment, his love of midcentury modern is on display everywhere, from the "Ours Polaire" Jean Royère sofa in the spare living room, to the Jean Prouvé chairs, to the wealth of art on the walls.

When it comes to books, however, the French-born de Bayser has more eclectic tastes altogether. "A mix of shit and quality." He smiles. "And I keep everything! Throw away a book? Never!" As such, Proust sits with Jojo Moyes, who lives next to *A Little Life*. De Bayser is interested in it all. "I usually carry two to three books with me, or you can get marooned. I bring something very easy, something a bit more difficult, and something in between, for my different moods." Then, too, it's useful to him as a retailer. "For my work, I need to understand what teenagers are thinking, what a woman may like, whether Romanticism is still in fashion."

Entering the apartment, one is faced with a room lined with deep bookshelves that reach almost to the sixteen-foot ceiling. Here is what qualifies as a working reference library on design and art, film and fashion, in book and monograph: everything one might ever wish to know about midcentury design, certainly, but also fiction in French and English and very occasionally German. Many are from his favorite Berlin bookstore, the nearby Dussmann. "I like to mix them," he explains. "It's much more interesting."

Aesthetics are important, of course; the books are intermingled carefully with small vases by Rick Owens, Georges Jouve ceramics, pieces by Alexandre Noll.

"THROW AWAY A
BOOK? NEVER!"

OPPOSITE The books are loosely organized by subject.

59

And de Bayser will readily admit to sacrificing substance for style—to a point. "To be honest, in Paris, I went to find several clothbound books in specific colors. The priority was the looks. But one is a special edition of Rilke. I happen to really like Rilke; it made sense *and* it was a beautiful green cover." He has also on occasion ventured into collecting books that also qualify as art: a set of Genet, for instance, designed by Giacometti— "two artists I love."

De Bayser says the Berlin apartment has allowed him to return to the pleasures of reading. "I was a very big reader when very young, but in this apartment, it's really a feeling of being home and now I need it, to wind down. I love to read in the evening in bed. Novels; I just want to escape." By his bed are *The Girls* by Emma Cline, a new novel by the British-Hungarian writer David Szalay, and *Chien-Loup*. "I would never read a book on a tablet—never, never. I'm on my phone all the time; this is my break."

On the subject of rereading, he is almost as emphatic. "I don't reread, I've never reread something." Then he considers. "I *would* reread Balzac—that meant so much to me. Proust is for when I've retired."

RIGHT The front door opens onto the library.

OPPOSITE A grouping of colorful objects bring whimsy to the bedroom.

OVERLEAF De Bayser's literary tastes are as varied as his interiors are purist.

"I WOULD NEVER
READ A BOOK
ON A TABLET—
NEVER, NEVER.
I'M ON MY PHONE
ALL THE TIME;
THIS IS MY BREAK."

THE BEAUTY
OF READING

PHILLIP LIM
New York, New York

"I DIDN'T START OUT AS A BOOK LOVER," admits Phillip Lim. "Initially, it was more about pragmatism: seeking knowledge having to do with research on work, on my interiors, building a home, even a word I wanted to understand more. But what I love about books is, once you start, you get to go deeper and deeper and deeper into a subject, and from there you go to another book, and another book, and soon after, you have a wall of books. And then you have two walls of books. And then—" The designer indicates the floor-to-ceiling bookcases that serve as the focal point of his loft apartment.

"Books are how I learn," Lim continues, "but I'm not nostalgic. I hate to look back; books inform you, but then they also become decoration. That may sound horrible to a true book lover, but I feel I honor them by making these objects part of my aesthetic world." The fact that the multicolored walls of spines are beautiful—as are many of the books themselves—is important to Lim's conception of his highly personal apartment.

Lim chose every element: the old-board floors, the custom birch bar, the limestone counters. "It's not for everyone," he concedes. "And it wouldn't necessarily be easy to sell. But it's my home; I built it for me, and books are the centerpiece."

His organizing principle is idiosyncratic. "They're strangely organized in my head, as I'd organize clothes, or organize interiors. They're not alphabetical, there's no color-coding, there's no system. Books about art would be next to interiors, interiors would be next to sofas. It's a visual kind of memory," he explains. "If I'm looking for Fortuny fabrics, I'll know that book is next to Louise Bourgeois, and, of course, she'll be next to Art Deco Mexican silver." He concedes that this system relies completely on his near-photographic memory, and that friends like to test him on the seemingly mysterious placement of the thousands of titles. He shudders at the

OVERLEAF The idiosyncratic organizational system is mysterious to everyone but Lim.

"BOOKS INFORM YOU, BUT THEN THEY ALSO BECOME DECORATION. THAT MAY SOUND HORRIBLE TO A TRUE BOOK LOVER, BUT I FEEL I HONOR THEM BY MAKING THESE OBJECTS PART OF MY AESTHETIC WORLD."

thought of a more conventional filing method: "I don't want another job! Books are for pleasure."

Surprisingly few of the titles have to do with fashion; Lim draws more inspiration from interiors books for "color schemes, shapes, silhouettes." While he doesn't believe in disposing of his books—"I acknowledge the storyline," as he puts it—he's grown more discerning in his many trips to bookstores like Dashwood on Bond Street, or Sag Harbor's Canio's Books. "With some experience, I understand what a good book is now. I've educated myself, and I'm more regimented."

That said, Lim loves to share books with friends, especially younger creatives who may not necessarily have a relationship with the printed page. Although we live in a social-media culture steeped in images, they are often presented without a larger context. "People forget the genesis—what came from what—and that's sad. You don't just get to know what you're looking at, but the context, the things around it." As to technology, "Ebooks are fine, but I like to underline, I like to hold a book." Lim always has two books in his bag, and although he admits his frenetic lifestyle makes it a challenge, he spends as much time as possible reading on the squishy sofa that faces his bookshelves.

"What I love is that now, friends will ask, hey, can I come spend the day in your house? They just want to come and look through the books. I warn them, if you sit there, you'll never leave; it's addicting."

ABOVE Although he does own fashion books (pictured), the bulk of Lim's library is devoted to art and design.

BELOW Lim's book collection has become famous among his friends; he's an enthusiastic lender.

69

ABOVE Phillip Lim in his New York apartment.

OPPOSITE Lim also appreciates books as decorative objects;
it's another way to honor them.

BOOKS FOR MILES

ALTHOUGH MANY OF NEW YORK'S BOOKSTORES have closed in recent years, the legendary Strand, boasting its fabled "18 Miles of Books," has since 1927 remained a proud standard-bearer for new, used, and rare books. In addition to being a reliable mecca for book lovers and a frequent host to author events, the Strand serves as a repository for the city's divestors: generations of New Yorkers— and more than a few publishing houses—have practically made a living selling the bookstore their castoffs. In addition to helping curate private libraries, the Strand is also a useful resource for set decorators and interior designers, who can, literally, buy books by the yard, not to mention, by color.

ABOVE The Strand's eighteen miles of books are a
New York City institution.

OPPOSITE Whether your poison's new or rare, golden, rose, or
teal, the Strand will have what you want.

THE LAYERS OF
A LIBRARY

ROMAN ALONSO

Los Angeles, California

ROMAN ALONSO IS NOT A MINIMALIST. As one might expect of one of the founders of Commune Design, the Venezuelan-born Alonso takes as eclectic and playful approach to his books as he does to the layered interiors of the hotels and homes for which the firm is known. "I don't really edit my library," he admits, "although I do give books from it as gifts to very special people all the time."

Most of Alonso's library is kept in what he calls his "reading nook," a shelf-filled room in his Los Angeles house that boasts a daybed, a colorful assortment of books and records, and a large balsa wood banana. And to judge by his books, his interests are wide ranging and often playful.

While there's an emphasis on design, there's also a good bit of biography, memoir, and history. "It's kind of like a bookstore," he says. "They're loosely organized by category: photography, film, counterculture, fashion, biographies, fiction, gay themes."

And while Alonso seems far from precious about his library, he does own a good number of rare editions. "I bought my first out-of-print, or collectible, books in 1994 from Arcana Books in Santa Monica," he says. "I got first editions of *Allure* by Diana Vreeland and *A Wonderful Time* by Slim Aarons, and those two got me started." He credits Arcana's Lee Kaplan, who is something of a local legend, with planting the seed. "I would say he is mostly responsible for starting my collection. I was working for Isaac Mizrahi at the time, and we would call Lee and ask him for books on Japan, or midcentury architecture, or whatever, and he would send us boxes of books and we'd return what we didn't want. It was before the Internet so he was this full-service book guy with great taste and knowledge of books who would send us stuff."

For all the beautiful art books and first editions, though, Alonso says it's the books with personal connections that he considers the most valuable. "My friend

OPPOSITE Whether pottery or books, everything in Roman
Alonso's collection has a personal meaning.

"I LOVE SPENDING
TIME IN MY READING
NOOK AT HOME,
BENEATH ALL MY
BOOKS, LOOKING
THROUGH THEM FOR
INSPIRATION."

ABOVE Roman Alonso in his Los Angeles
living room.

LEFT Many of the most beloved books were
gifts from friends.

OPPOSITE Alonso credits independent
bookstores—especially L.A.'s Arcana—for most
of his collection, which is as layered as the décor.

OVERLEAF Alonso's favorite "reading nook,"
which he misses when he travels.

Amy Spindler gave me two out-of-print Anita Loos books when I moved to Los Angeles, *A Girl Like I* and *Kiss Hollywood Goodbye*. I treasure them because a couple of years later Amy died of brain cancer, and she was a huge influence on me when I moved to L.A. to start a new life." Another favorite is a copy of Mercedes de Acosta's bio, *Here Lies the Heart*. "She was Greta Garbo's lover. The book belonged to Gavin Lambert, who I knew when I first moved to L.A. and was Nicholas Ray's lover. My friend Konstantin Kakanias got Gavin's entire book collection when he died, and Konstantin gave me the book as a gift, to remember Gavin by."

Although the reading nook—and indeed the house—is already bursting with beloved hardcovers, Alonso seems in no rush to stop the influx.

"I love going to bookstores. I will shop online for reference books I use at work, but going to a bookstore to look for books is one of my favorite things to do. And I have my favorite bookstores in different cities that I visit religiously when I'm there. In Los Angeles, Arcana is still my favorite. In New York I love Dashwood Books, and Mast books is a new favorite. I love Comptoir de L'Image in Paris. And the best architecture and design bookstore is William Stout in San Francisco."

All this travel, of course, leaves ample time for reading, and Alonso says that's when he gets through the most books. But "I love spending time in my reading nook at home, beneath all my books, looking through them for inspiration. They are like old friends to me, and I miss them when I don't visit them."

THE DRAWING LIFE

JOANA AVILLEZ
New York, New York

"BEFORE I LIVED IN MY DAD'S STUDIO, I had a really tight grip on my books," says illustrator and author Joana Avillez of the library in her bright TriBeCa loft. "I was always pruning and organizing, and when making a new addition, I would present it to the members of the shelf for feedback and acceptance on both subject and placement. Now the library is the merging of two already merged people." The loft was originally the office of her father, the late artist Martim Avillez, and the base of his arts journal *Lusitania*. It was her father who built much of the space's functional, minimalist furniture—the sawhorse dining table, the hidden cupboards, the many built-in bookcases. The result is a space that feels intensely personal, hypercreative, and filled with an uncluttered dynamism.

Her Murphy bed is set into one of these walls of bookshelves, clearly indicating the importance of reading in the artist's daily routine. "I sleep surrounded by my books," says Avillez. "I find it comforting." The library itself is a combination of Avillez's own collection of novels, history, and art theory and those she inherited from her father. She arranges the books, roughly, by subject. "My dad's art and theory and culture books and my illustration and cartooning and children's books—our collection overlaps at comics (he knew his

> "I LIKE TO HAVE ALL MY FAVORITES IN MY SIGHTLINE."

stuff). I've had to move some of the Deleuze and Guattari and Spinoza biographies a bit higher up—I like to have all my favorites in my sightline (like picture books about animals living in stumps)."

Avillez loves children's books, which she draws on for inspiration: Barbara Cooney, Tintin, Beatrix Potter, Ludwig Bemelmans. "My plumber once asked me how many kids I had based on my colorful and largely fonted library," says Avillez, who has has none.

On her shelves and walls, books—many French and Portuguese, reflecting her family's varied origins—mingle with art. Avillez's own work—mostly inspired by

OPPOSITE Avillez's father built her book-enclosed Murphy bed when the apartment was his art studio.

81

the energy of her home city—keeps company with sculptures by her father, a Milena Pavlović-Barili portrait of her grandmother, and works by Leah Reena Goren, Dike Blair, and Joan Jonas. "Because the space is limited," she says, "I really have to confine my collections of things, clothes, and especially books to those I truly love, or that have great sentimental value." She likes best to borrow. "I'm always asking for recommendations," she says, "and I take very good care of my friends' books!"

Part of the problem is that Avillez never knows what she might draw on for inspiration. Recently, for instance, while coming up with a "character" for a fashion brand, she felt a strong desire to look at a certain image from Helmut Newton's *Portraits*—luckily easily accessible via her rolling library ladder. Collaborating on Julia Sherman's *Salad for President,* she immersed herself in cookbooks. When designing wallpaper for the clubhouse of The Wing, she read biographies of iconic women. And certain references are perennials: back issues of the *New Yorker, Eloise,* the work of cartoonists like Garth Williams.

"Depending on what I'm working on," she says, "I always have a few books on my worktable," which is an organized space made of scavenged filing cabinets and filled with pencils, pens, colorful watercolors. Lately she has surrounded herself with the books of William Steig to help inform her phonetic puzzle book, *DC-T!* that she collaborated on with writer Molly Young. Now, Steig's *CDB!* holds pride of place next to *Tintin* and a memoir about an early-twentieth-century artists' colony, and a 1940s YA novel appropriately titled *Betty Loring, Illustrator,* which was a gift from a friend.

When reading for pleasure, Avillez usually stretches on the forest-green daybed near the loft's series of large windows. "Because this is essentially one room," she says, "I like to try to kind of divide it by activity; it keeps you sane—and organized—to leave 'work' at the end of the day." Often, she'll take a book with her to the park where she walks her feisty terrier mix, Pepito (named after a character in Ludwig Bemelmans's *Madeline* series) and read while he plays in the small-dogs' run.

OPPOSITE Joana Avillez with a portrait of her grandmother.

ABOVE Avillez loves the work of fellow New Yorker Ludwig Bemelmans.

OVERLEAF The books are shelved by subject, mostly.

BOOK PERFUME

CECILIA BEMBIBRE LIVES WITH HER NOSE IN A BOOK—professionally. The Brazilian-born Bembibre left a publishing career to study the science of scent, specifically heritage scent, a discipline devoted to distilling the aromas of human experience. "Training is a lot," she says, "it's about looking at the connections between brain and nose." While ultimately Bembibre and her colleagues will isolate a range of heritage smells, "The smell of books was one of the first case studies," she explains. Her lab attempts to break down not merely the chemistry of aromas but also the associations.

One of the subjects is the library of Knoll, the 365-room "calendar house" that has been owned by the same family since the fifteenth century (and that, incidentally, served as an inspiration for Virginia Woolf's *Orlando*). There is tremendous variety, depending on bindings and shelving. "Older books are less acid," she explains. And while, in their distillation, "most of the archetypal compounds exist . . . I'd not claim to have captured all books." Still, the vial of laboratory-distilled book dust she uncorks is just that: the pure essence of paper and vellum, leather and ink, and time. "People think of the smell of books as the smell of language," Bembibre says. "Wisdom that you can inhale."

ABOVE Knoll is a "calendar house," containing 365 rooms, one for each day of the year.

OPPOSITE Cecilia Bembibre searches for the essence of a book from Knoll's library.

A BEAUTIFUL
MESS

IRENE SILVAGNI
Arles, France

IRENE SILVAGNI STILL GETS EMOTIONAL when she recalls the flood that overran her eighteenth-century home fifteen years ago. "The courtyard was filled with ruined books—more than two hundred," recalls the fashion editor and former creative director for Yohji Yamamoto. "We cried."

Many, however, survived, and in the years since, Silvagni's large library of fashion, film, and art books has been amply replenished. Like the rest of the home, the books are arranged with both a careful curatorial eye and an instinctive confidence: no surprise, given the inclinations of both Silvagni and her late husband, film producer Giorgio, whom she credits for much of the décor.

Today, Silvagni shares the home with her widowed daughter-in-law. The sprawling stone house she has lived in for the better part of thirty years is set in a van Gogh landscape of sunflower fields, farms, and dusty dirt roads. In the casually lovely garden, iron daybeds invite lounging and reading under the trees. "The garden is like me, disordered," says Silvagni, who, far from the stereotype of the domineering editrix, is warm and quietly authoritative. "But I like a bit of mess."

The hum of cicadas is everywhere—but so is Top 40; Silvagni is addicted to French MTV and has it playing in every room where she works. Similarly, the house itself combines traditional Provençal elements—couches strewn with vintage ticking cushions, wrought iron salvaged from the bull rings of nearby Arles, tilework, jewel-toned *boutis* quilts—with classics of modernist design. "My husband was Italian," she explains with a smile. "So—the Italian furniture. His father was a decorator, and he inherited a wonderful sense of color. And, of course, we both loved books and reading, so they are in every room."

The arrangement of the books is seemingly casual but never haphazard; whether it is the wall of bookcases above Silvagni's preferred sofa or the stacks in the airy

OPPOSITE "I'm a bit messy," says Silvagni of her arranging strategy.

89

ABOVE LEFT Soft colors set off art and photography books in a bedroom.

ABOVE RIGHT Decades of magazines on an antique mail cart.

LEFT French novels and matelassé curtains in a bedroom.

OPPOSITE In her home office, Silvagni's favorite books are mixed with photographs from throughout her career.

bedrooms. Like everything else, the collection is eclectic: Contemporary novels keep company with French classics, film history, and photography. Silvagni knows where everything is.

And, of course, there are magazines. In the living room, antique post office carts hold decades' worth of *Vogue, Look, Habitué,* and *Va Bene*. A taxidermied grizzly is perched atop one; "I went shopping for flowers and came back with a bear," explains Silvagni.

The walls also pay testament to Silvagni's storied career; while editing French *Vogue*, she is known for having pioneered the work of photographers like Peter Lindbergh, Steven Meisel, Bruce Weber, and Paolo Roversi, and everywhere hang lovingly inscribed portraits and iconic layouts, as well as family snapshots and work by Silvagni's daughter.

While discussing her current bedside reading, *Le Mort de Louis XV,* Silvagni is arrested by the opening bars of a song by the French-Congolese trap artist Gradur. "Oh, turn it up!" she says excitedly. "I love this song!" For Silvagni, there's no conflict; only inspiration.

ABOVE LEFT Irene Silvagni in her bedroom.

ABOVE RIGHT A selection of novels, philosophy, and fashion by the bedside.

OPPOSITE The home is a mixture of local antiques, family history, and souvenirs of travel.

OVERLEAF In a bedroom, genres, styles, and colors mix beautifully.

CHILD'S PLAY

"THEY'RE FASCINATING AS HISTORY, of course, but also so beautiful as art objects," says Clare Simms of her collection of movable books. These include eighteenth-century pull-tab books, instructive Victorian "turn-up books," and the wealth of nineteenth-century three-dimensional and moving-parts children's books created by Ernest Nister and Lothar Meggendorfer, as well as the iconic Bookano pop-ups from the 1950s. The Victorian era gave birth to tunnel or peep-show books—one of Simms's represents a scale model of the Crystal Palace—and they served as popular souvenirs.

Her collection ranges from the whimsical (dogs with pull-tab wagging tongues) to the frightening (turn-ups that end with a skeleton in a grave). Because so many were intended as playthings, it's amazing that any have survived intact. But, says Simms, "I quite like the authenticity if it's a bit scuffed, or if one of the tabs doesn't work . . . I consider that to be part of the interest." That said, she has firmly barred her two young sons from the antique books: "They have so many modern pop-ups we *don't* need to be precious about!"

ABOVE An early instructional folding-book.

OPPOSITE A Victorian tunnel book.

WONDER, CURIOSITY, AND STRANGE DREAMS

VIK MUNIZ
Brooklyn, New York

"I CANNOT LIVE WITHOUT A LIBRARY, and I cannot live without a garden," says Vik Muniz. "A garden is where we negotiate with nature—a place between the wild and the tame—and a library is where we confront everything." In his Brooklyn studio, he can do both: One wall is devoted to thousands of books, another, made of glass, looks out onto lush greenery.

The Brazilian artist is known for his range of inspirations and media, as well as his use of pop culture and media imagery, so it's perhaps not surprising that the studio has something of an air of a postmodern cabinet of curiosities, where scrimshaw, shells, arrowheads, a Jeff Koons dog, and a massive pair of scissors live with the books on the shelves.

"I'm very messy," Muniz says cheerfully. The books, he explains, are organized "like heat maps, I would say. There's no obvious organization, but I sort of know how they connect. Sometimes I like to climb up and down the ladder, just to see if I can find something." Despite the huge number of books, Muniz says he wouldn't call himself a collector as such. "I grew up poor. And poor people have a hard time throwing things away."

While Muniz keeps his fiction and poetry at his family home in Brazil, this one "is more of a technical library; most of it is related to psychology or philosophy. Reference and inspiration." At the moment, he's reading a great deal of the mystics Gurdjieff and Ouspensky, Blavatsky, Edwin Abbott's *Flatland*, William James, as well as the quixotic seventeenth-century polymath Athanasius Kircher. That's

> "MY BOOKS ARE LIKE HEAT MAPS, I WOULD SAY. THERE'S NO OBVIOUS ORGANIZATION, BUT I SORT OF KNOW HOW THEY CONNECT."

OPPOSITE Muniz "cannot live without a library, and . . . without a garden."

99

"SOMETIMES I
LIKE TO CLIMB UP
AND DOWN THE
LADDER JUST TO
SEE IF I CAN
FIND SOMETHING."

to say nothing of astrophysics, alchemy, and Euclidean geometry. In short: He's interested in the whole of human development. "Wonder, curiosity, strange dreams: That's what I like," he says. "Ovid's *Metamorphoses* is another book that I love."

When he does read fiction, he says, "I like books where people describe reading": Luis Sepulveda's *The Old Man Who Read Love Stories*; Italo Calvino's *Why Read the Classics*; Borges's *Library of Babel.* "I start many things and I can't finish anything," he says. "I go home and my daughter is reading four books at once! And she's twelve!"

Yet, no one can doubt the scope of his curiosity or the breadth of his interests. The thousands of books that surround him make up a working library in the truest sense of the word. As Muniz explains his philosophy, "Man's development—our relationship with facts—is all about communicating between the mental and material. I still see the page as the best tool for that."

RIGHT This Brooklyn library is devoted purely to nonfiction; poetry and novels are in Brazil.

ABOVE Vik Muniz in his Brooklyn studio.

OPPOSITE "I can never find anything!" says Muniz.

Bart's Books
OPEN
7 Days A Week
9:30-SUNSET
When Closed
Please throw coins in slot
in the door for the amount
marked on the book.
Thank You
STAR TREK AND PHILOSOPHY
GRIM CITY
BEATING THE STREET
Sunnyside

BART'S BOOKS

BART'S BOOKS IN OJAI, CALIFORNIA, has been called "the greatest outdoor bookstore in the world," and it's certainly among the most idiosyncratic. "Founded" in 1964, the shop was originally a set of shelves on a sidewalk holding Richard Bartinsdale's excess books; money was left by donation in coffee cans. Even as the sprawling, bohemian store has grown into one of the finest independent bookstores in America, the honor system continues (to a point) to this day. So does Bart's relaxed vibe—both indoors and outdoors.

ABOVE An Ojai institution with a So-Cal attitude.

OPPOSITE The shop has maintained its casual, quirky hours.

the ARRANGERS

THE LAST LIBRARY

LARRY MCMURTRY
Archer City, Texas

Growing up on a family ranch outside the town of Archer City, Texas, Larry McMurtry recalls that the family told one another stories by necessity: They owned no books. The prolific author has been making up for it ever since; in addition to his own large body of work—which includes *The Last Picture Show, Lonesome Dove, Terms of Endearment,* and the screenplay to *Brokeback Mountain*—he is the owner of a virtual town's worth of volumes. Indeed, in Archer City, books outnumber people by a good margin.

"My earliest encounter with books came when I was six years old," he says. "My cousin Robert Hilbern came to me when he was on his way to World War II and left me nineteen volumes of boy's books. Some were from the Poppy Ott series"— boys' action stories—"and the others were from the Jerry Todd adventures and Sergeant Silk the Prairie Scout."

While studying at Stanford, McMurtry first became a rare-book scout and later put this expertise to use as the manager or owner of some twenty-six bookshops. The most famous, Houston's Bookman, in turn, migrated to Washington, D.C., where McMurtry opened Georgetown's Booked Up. The final iteration of Booked Up is bibliophilic legend: a four-warehouse, 450,000-volume used bookstore in McMurtry's hometown of Archer City. Despite periodic threats of closure and a massive 2012 offloading of inventory known as The Last Booksale, the shop's footprint continues to mark Archer City irrevocably.

> "OF COURSE I DIP INTO MY OWN STORE; I CHOSE THE BOOKS IN MY STORE MYSELF, AND SO THEY INTEREST ME."

While the "personal" collection McMurtry shares with his wife, Faye, fills their home, in fact, the books move regularly between house and Booked Up's

OPPOSITE While the library's range is vast, obviously it contains a deep Western section.

PREVIOUS PAGES McMurtry's home library displays the discipline of a longtime bookseller.

OVERLEAF "I read every day," says McMurtry.

sprawling facilities. "Of course I read books from my store!" he says. The home library is as organized as any bookstore: In the house, the books are organized by subject; a small structure behind the main house holds both McMurtry's notable collection of women's travel writing and his vast reference library on western subjects.

Despite his recent divestiture—McMurtry didn't want to saddle his heirs with the massive library in the era of Amazon—there are books he'd never sell. "Nathanael West's four novels would be ones I wouldn't part with: *The Dream Life of Balso Snell*; *Miss Lonelyhearts*; *A Cool Million: The Dismantling of Lemuel Pitkin*; and *The Day of the Locust*. Other than those volumes, my library is, you might say, 'a vibrant intellectual ecosystem.'"

ABOVE The line between shop and home can be porous, as there are books that interest him. McMurtry reads a great deal from the stock.

OPPOSITE, ABOVE Booked Up is an Archer City landmark.

OPPOSITE, BELOW A corner of the store.

ABOVE A legend of the modern west.

OPPOSITE Despite a famous "last booksale," McMurtry's
personal collection is massive.

AN OASIS
OF ORDER

TODD HIDO
San Francisco, California

I F TODD HIDO'S COLLECTION IS NOT the most extensive private photography library in America, it is certainly the most systemized. "All 6,241 volumes are cataloged," he explains. "The organizing system is based on theme, grouped by the type of photography the photographers do: schools of thought, lineage from photographer to assistant or photographer to student. Nothing is in alphabetical order."

Despite the idiosyncratic methodology, the library in the photographer's Arts and Crafts San Francisco house has an air of great professionalism, from the "book room" sign lettered on the glass panel of the door, to the mission oak study table and chairs, to the rotating display of volumes that Hido periodically displays face-out on the shelves. With a few exceptions—Hido's notable and colorful collection of mid-century pulp, for instance—the books are dedicated to photography and film, and the collection is both deep and varied.

Hido himself, known for moody shots of interiors and exteriors of houses, is an accomplished author: To date there exists some sixteen monographs of his works.

Although Hido says he was an indifferent student, his love of books goes back a long way, starting with a single formative volume. "It was from my first teacher in college and it was *The Americans* by Robert Frank." He still has it.

From there, Hido's course was set. He's been collecting books steadily, from the classics of the genre—Frank, Henri Cartier-Bresson, Walker Evans—to the rare; first editions of Ed Ruscha and Irving Penn. Hido also has a comprehensive collection of his contemporaries' work, and that of prominent fashion and film

"I'VE ALWAYS BEEN A PERSON WHO ARRANGES THINGS. IT'S ALMOST LIKE THIS OBSESSIVE HABIT I HAVE."

OPPOSITE Todd Hido's home library, with books on a rotating display.

117

photographers, and is perpetually haunting book-shops in search of new acquisitions—which then, in turn, must be cataloged and shelved according to the system.

At any given moment, Hido explains, a few special books will be out for perusal, depending on his mood, interests, and inspiration. Right now, *Photo Books in Sweden* and the Gerhard Richter's *Atlas* are in the spotlight. Hido has always been an arranger. "Is there any other way to be?" he asks. "My environment is incredibly important to me. Arranging things creates order, not just in your own space but also in all of life."

ABOVE Films, books, prints—a shrine to the media.

BELOW The mission oak bones of the house set off the photography.

OPPOSITE Todd Hido at home in San Francisco.

"ARRANGING THINGS CREATES ORDER, NOT JUST IN YOUR OWN SPACE BUT ALSO IN ALL OF LIFE."

ABOVE Vintage lighting equipment in the studio.

BELOW Hido's own work is revered for its distinctive lighting and composition.

OPPOSITE Books are systematically cataloged and shelved.

DEWEY DECIMAL BY DESIGN

UNIVERSITY LIBRARIES ARE, PERHAPS, the hardest-working of all: the spaces need to provide function as well as storage and, whenever possible, comfort. While they range from grand to minimal, baroque to bare bones, all require a particular mix of sense and sensibility. The largest open-stack library in Germany, the Grimm Zentrum library at Berlin's Humboldt University, was completed in 2009 and is decidedly contemporary. But the marble exterior, slitted façade, and central gallery were based upon Friedrich Schinkel's 1833 plans. Like the collection of over two million books, the library itself is a collection of old and new, functional and philosophical.

ABOVE The collection contains over two million books.

OPPOSITE, ABOVE The Grimm Zentrum library at Berlin's Humboldt
University is the largest open-stack library in Germany.

OPPOSITE, BELOW The library was completed in 2009.

DESIGN FOR READING

MARK LEE

Los Angeles, California

THE L.A.-BASED MARK LEE—who is one-half of the firm Johnston Marklee along with partner Sharon Johnston—has recently become bicoastal: as chair of the Harvard Graduate School of Design, Lee now spends part of his year in Cambridge, Massachusetts.

While Johnston Marklee is acclaimed for the versatility of its designs—the firm has done a wide range of projects all over the world, including museum additions, galleries, homes, and stores—their aesthetic could be called both minimal and arresting, somehow lush and pared down at the same time.

The same is true of Lee's library, which is a mixture of architecture and design, art, fashion, and literature, and is forever evolving. Says Lee, "I once read an Umberto Eco quote, whose gist was some people treat libraries like mausoleums, but libraries should be alive. And I agree. I always have a dynamic relationship with my books."

The library in his Los Angeles home is a bibliophile's dream, as well as a design enthusiast's. Despite its clean lines, it's colorful, layered, and comfortable, with earthy textiles, art, and whimsical lamps that add warmth and personality. In the studio, an elevated gallery contains the library, where small, convenient lights fall over elegant chairs, and at every shelf, one is encouraged to browse, sit, and read in understated comfort. "I have about five hundred shelves of books," he calculates. "It probably comes to about twenty thousand," of which Lee estimates he's read seventy percent.

Lee has compiled the books over the past thirty-three years. "Everyone has their first love," says Lee. "For me, it was the collected works of Le Corbusier. I bought it in architecture school,

"THERE'S SOMETHING ABOUT THE PHYSICAL BOOK, THE ART OF TURNING THE PAGE, THAT'S INHERENTLY COMFORTING, AND I'M AN ARCHITECT, SO I VALUE THE PHYSICAL."

and I still have the same edition. That's what started my book collection, and I've been adding to it ever since." And his methods haven't changed. "I do it the old-fashioned way: I go to bookstores. I count on the booksellers' curation to suggest new books." Although many of his favorite bookshops have closed, Lee remains a devotee of the L.A. art bookshops Hennessey and Ingalls and Arcana: Books on the Arts. Of the latter, he explains that proprietor Lee Kaplan's occasional annotation adds to the experience. "Lee adds comments on the flyleaf—notes on a book's importance or provenance—that's like a historical lesson," he enthuses.

While he's not a major editor of his voluminous book collection, Lee says that occasionally he's prone to forgetting what he owns and buying duplicates, which he then passes on to friends. "Books are such great gifts, because they don't just say what you think about the book, but about the person you're giving them to."

Despite the demanding nature of his schedule, Lee is a voracious reader. "I read everywhere," he says. "I have a great reading chair, and I read in bed—a terrible habit for my neck and my eyes. But I find it calming: It's a different part of my brain, unlike the way I take in other media, and I think I retain information better."

ABOVE Being an architect, says Lee, gives him an appreciation
for the book as a physical object.

OPPOSITE Mark Lee at home in Los Angeles.

OVERLEAF Lee has been amassing his collection since he arrived in Los Angeles.

A SPACE
FOR IDEAS

JONATHAN SAFRAN FOER
Brooklyn, New York

"I'VE BUILT IT UP IN FITS AND STARTS," says novelist Jonathan Safran Foer of his library. And it is, indeed, a true library: a dedicated room of his own design filled with purpose-built navy-blue bookshelves, a large Liberty-print sofa, soft white rug, and vintage light fixtures embellished with cast iron birds. Like the rest of the Brooklyn Victorian, it's inviting and homey; cushioned window seats, a special nook for his children to curl up in, large living room sofas, and good lamps encourage reading all over the house. The writer, however, uses the library for its intended purpose.

"I really only read in the library," he says. "I'm really attached to the idea that different spaces, whether physical or interpersonal, will create different thoughts and experiences. Having a comfortable chair, good light—these things do put you into a state of mind to better absorb ideas."

Foer's diverse book collection, which spans classics, modern fiction, art, biography, and reference for various projects, started in his early twenties. "I was living on a farm in New Jersey after I graduated college," he explains, "and I'd often go to library sales on the weekends. That was the basis, and I keep most things."

Nowadays, he shops at the Strand, and at Unnameable Books in nearby Prospect Heights; new books he tends to buy at the McNally Jackson bookstore in SoHo. However, while he's quick to praise these stores, he adds: "New York is not a great book town, oddly enough." He prefers the shopping near his hometown, of Washington, D.C. "When I go home, I'll often go to a warehouse in Rockville, Maryland: Second Story Books. I pick up a lot there, and, often, entire sets of books."

On those rare occasions when he does divest, Foer has built a small wooden lending library that he puts out on the street, encouraging neighbors to give and take. It's a sight seen occasionally in Brooklyn, and regularly in D.C.—an unobtrusive bit of neighborly interaction.

OPPOSITE Foer's library.

131

While he retains those books he loves, of course, Foer also believes in surrounding himself with books he hasn't yet read, a sort of literary optimism. "I once read Umberto Eco say something about walking among books you *might* one day read, and I love that idea. Especially with novels, but also art books." By his own admission, his family life, work, and the associated directed reading, limits the amount of time he has to read for pleasure. But the library remains a beacon.

And while reading in situ may have a philosophical impetus, it's also practical: "The older I get, the more impossible I find it to read in bed," he says. "I fall asleep immediately."

"HAVING A COMFORTABLE CHAIR, GOOD LIGHT—THESE THINGS DO PUT YOU INTO A STATE OF MIND TO BETTER ABSORB IDEAS."

ABOVE Jonathan Safran Foer at home in Brooklyn.

OPPOSITE Books, read and unread, tempt in the living room.

ABOVE Foer loves the idea of living with books you *might* read.

OPPOSITE Writers' letterheads on the bathroom wall.

A COMMON
THREAD

JORDANA MUNK MARTIN
Brooklyn, New York

J ORDANA MUNK MARTIN'S LIBRARY IS HER LEGACY. Literally: After the death of her grandmother Edith Wyle, the American folk artist, Martin inherited not just her collection of more than a thousand books about the textile arts, but also her passion to share the knowledge in those books with the larger world. "When she started her collection, material culture—weaving, quilting, sewing—wasn't part of the conversation. These things were considered a feminine sphere and were somewhat marginalized. But she loved craft; the moment when something functional becomes beautiful."

According to family lore, Edith Wyle decided to become a gallerist when a back injury put her in traction. Unable to paint, Edith decided to collect instead: she began to assemble examples of handicrafts along with books about these crafts she loved so much. What started as the Egg and the Eye Gallery in 1965 grew into Los Angeles's Craft & Folk Art Museum in 1973. Traditionally feminine disciplines like weaving, quilting, and sewing had not been considered "art" before Edith's generation. She sought to legitimize and highlight these skills, and also curate their written record: She began to collect as many books as she could find on the subject of textiles.

Jordana Martin grew up using her grandmother's library functionally: to learn about weaving, tatting, bobbin lace—all the lost arts of textile manufacture. An artist herself, Martin was fascinated by the same things that had captured her grand-mother: the history and lore of cloth, and the woven-in, hidden conversations with craftswomen and makers over centuries.

For years after her grandmother's death, Martin admits she didn't know exactly what to do with the massive library of textile books she had inherited. But when, in 2016, she was gifted with the collection of another textile-obsessed bibliophile

OPPOSITE A library where books and fabrics are given equal respect.

OVERLEAF Martin loves the symbolism and rich cross-cultural
history of the color blue.

137

named Carol Westfall, the size of her library doubled. Her destiny was clear: Martin wanted to make these conversations available to others. She formed TATTER, a library composed completely of books on textiles. In the years since she founded it, Martin has worked with a librarian to catalog the ever-growing collection and has created a serene, remarkable space where visitors can arrange to borrow and study the more than three thousand books. Of the decision to put her family's legacy on display, Martin says it was obvious. "Really, it's always been about people learning from each other," she says. "I was so fortunate to be able to bring my history and my passions together; of course I wanted to share it."

What she's created is remarkable. Despite the formal catalog and trained archivists, TATTER is by no means a conventional library; it is an experience. Inconspicuously located in an industrial building above Brooklyn's Textile Arts Center, the exterior gives no hint of the riches hidden inside. Walk in, and you might think you've stumbled upon an art installation, or perhaps an exclusive atelier. For one thing, the space is blue. *Very* blue. Wonderfully, completely, overwhelmingly blue, from walls to bookshelves to the indigo-dyed kimonos and objects that dot the room. There is nothing retiring about this color; it's the hue of uniforms and skies and flags. The color has always drawn Martin (who wears blue-framed glasses). "I've always collected blue objects, since I can remember," she says. She credits her parents' love of the Japanese arts for exposing her to their textiles and pottery at an early age, but the

ABOVE LEFT A serene grouping of handmade pottery in Martin's home.

ABOVE RIGHT The one rule for books in the house—nothing gets shelved.

OPPOSITE The house skews more white than blue.

Claus Goedicke　　　Dinge　　　Schirmer/Mosel

TIM WALKER　PICTURES　teNeues

Irving Penn　　Still Life　　Bulfinch

SEEING IS FORGETTING THE NAME OF THE THING ONE SEES　CALIFORNIA

MARTIN PURYEAR　THE ART INSTITUTE OF CHICAGO　THAMES AND HUDSON

HESS ART COLLECTION　HATJE CANTZ

HANDCRAFTED MAINE

HANDWOVEN TAPE　Schiffer

E　Makoto AZUMA　Shunsuke SHIINOKI
ENCYCLOPEDIA OF FLOWERS　II

TOSHIKO TAKAEZU

THE WHITE ROAD　EDMUND DE WAAL

Ottolenghi & Goh　　SWEET

"IT'S NOT THE BIGGEST COLLECTION OF TEXTILE BOOKS IN THE WORLD, BUT IT'S CERTAINLY THE MOST PERSONAL."

fascination is philosophical, too. "I love the global authority of blue," she explains. "It's used universally, it's so much a part of the natural world, and yet it was one of the last colors to be named. So much of blue is in how it's perceived."

As one's eyes adjust to the blueness, you perceive not just the thousands of volumes—textile history, antique instructional manuals, catalogs—but the many objects Martin also considers part of the library: bobbins and looms, framed textiles and spindles. The effect is holistic, what Martin calls "a gathering of material culture." TATTER, she explains, is about telling stories, "and cloth is the hero."

Whatever its curated beauty, however, TATTER is a functioning circulating library; anyone can make an appointment to visit and lose an afternoon or a few weeks immersing themselves in the world of textile books. "It's not the biggest collection of textile books in the world," says Martin, "but it's certainly the most personal."

In the light-filled nearby brownstone that Martin shares with her husband and two sons, these personal stories continue. There are books stacked in fireplaces and on windowsills, by bathtubs and forming free-form tables. Books are everywhere. But the one thing you *won't* find is bookshelves. "At home, I live with books very much as I do objects," she explains. The home is largely, although not completely, blue; the second house the family owns in Maine is, says Martin, even bluer.

In both house and library—the collection often moves between the two—books are treated with respect but not awe; just as Martin learned to craft from her grandmother's books, now she hopes others will come not just to read but also

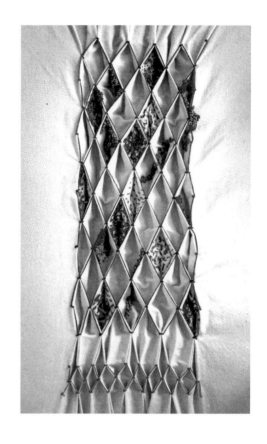

to absorb. "So much of this is a conversation," she says. "I never met Carol Westfall, but I feel like I know her through her books. And I feel connected to my grandmother every day." Asked to name her favorite book, Martin, after running her fingers along shelves filled with beloved titles and weighty tomes, pulls a slim, unassuming volume from the wall: a catalog called *Blue Traditions*. It was, she explains, a book that was independently owned by both her grandmother and Carol Westfall. "Clearly, it meant so much to these two women, and of course to me. And it's blue! It's a dialogue," says Martin, "between women; between eras; between books—which are, after all, made of cloth—and objects."

ABOVE An example of deep smocking in Martin's collection of needlework.

OPPOSITE Jordana Munk Martin at home.

THE·LANDING·OF·CABRILLO·AT·CATALINA

A LIBRARY LEADS THE WAY

PUBLIC LIBRARIES HAVE LONG SERVED as community hubs where neighbors can gather around their love of books; now they are increasingly becoming refuges with technological resources to serve *everyone* in the community. In recent years, the Los Angeles Public Library, which serves a larger population than any public library system in the United States, has gone even further. They've instituted a public wireless network that students who do not have Internet access can "check out" and use in their own homes, however remote, twenty-four hours a day.

The buildings themselves serve as both a gathering space and something of a civic center: In addition to providing services for veterans, continuing education, ESL, adult literacy, and those who are homeless, the LAPL provides a range of resources for immigrants. At branches around the city, the New Americans Centers and New Americans Welcome Stations help people learn their legal rights, find information on guardianship services and entrepreneurship, and get help filing paperwork.

ABOVE Public libraries—and books—bring communities together.

OPPOSITE The LAPL: a meeting of old California and the contemporary world.

THE COMIC LIFE

ART SPIEGELMAN & FRANÇOISE MOULY
SoHo, New York

"THE FIRST THING YOU NEED TO UNDERSTAND," says Art Spiegelman, gesturing to the thousands of books that line the walls of the loft, "is that Françoise and I have quite different tastes."

"It's true," adds his wife, Françoise Mouly. "There is overlap, of course," she adds. "I mean, we do both love comics."

This is an understatement: the pair could be called comics royalty. Spiegelman is the Pulitzer-winning author of *Maus;* Mouly, an accomplished comics writer in her own right, is the longtime art editor of *The New Yorker.* They cofounded the seminal comics magazine *Raw* and later became the publishers of Raw Books and Toon Books, helping to establish graphic novels as a serious art form. For more than twenty years, they—and their library—have lived in a rambling apartment in New York's SoHo neighborhood.

The space has the air of the "old" SoHo, when the neighborhood was filled with artists and creatives rather than chain stores; it's not just the series of cozy, lived-in rooms that create the impression, but also the vast profusion of memorabilia, family photographs, and well-read volumes.

Bookshelves fill the walls of each of the apartment's rooms: living room, dining room, loft. Whatever real estate isn't taken up by books is given over to comics art: the covers of the pair's own work, as well as original black-and-white Fleischer cartoon stills, R. Crumb drawings, and the iconic 9/11 *New Yorker* cover on which they collaborated.

Spiegelman keeps most of his comics collection in his memorabilia-jammed study—"because then I know exactly where everything is, more or less"—whether that's an 1880s Buster Brown compendium or a new French graphic novel, called a *bande dessinée*. However, neither one retains many of the comics from their childhoods: "Both Françoise and I learned to read by reading comics. But we sacrificed our own prized comic book collection to our kids, so that they could learn to read from

OPPOSITE A book-filled corner in the family's book-filled apartment.

them as well." The office is a virtual museum to the history of comics and cartooning. "Comics are a narrative art form, a form that combines two other forms of expression: words and pictures," says Spiegelman, pulling down rare early comics, vintage *Mad* magazines. Good comics make an impression that lasts forever." He displays 1940s instructional manuals, 1930s Listerine ads. "Classic American comic strips have conviction and innocence. They are built around strong storytelling. All that is left are superheroes. Before the comic book crash that was brought about by McCarthy's council on un-American actitivies, there were even comic book phonics textbooks for kids."

Mouly's favorite books—and shelves—tend to be more minimal. "There's a certain kind of comic aesthetic that is chock-full, you know, very *Mad* magazine, with a million different details. Art is more tolerant of this. I can be brought to tears by a few simple lines." She pulls a vintage copy of *Otto's Orange Day*—an early Toon Book—from its place. "To me design and printing are important. For Art these are a means to an end. I love making things. Art makes things because that's something he has to do in order to express his ideas. I don't have ideas outside of making things. I can't do what he does, expounding on the theory of this and that. I'm like, 'Can I just show you, and not have to tell?' Maybe it's because I'm operating in a second language."

Less expected is the couple's extensive collection of fairy tales, a major influence on both artists. An entire dining room shelf is devoted to the Brothers Grimm, Arthur Rackham, and Disney, explains Mouly, "Children recognize their own experiences in the paradigms presented in fairy tales. Kids may not have a lot of experience, but they've got a wealth of very complex feelings and emotions and ideas running through their heads."

Spiegelman has a passion for children's books, too. "I would say that the Carl Barks's *Donald Duck* comics are great, great kids' books. They love them. They're exceptionally well-crafted stories." He pulls comics from the shelves as he talks. "And *Little Lulu* is especially good and would work very well now because the stories are

"I OFTEN FEEL WE ARE DROWNING IN OUR BOOKS. HOW MUCH MORE CAN WE FIT IN? BUT HOW CAN WE STOP? THIS IS WHAT WE DO, HOW WE LIVE."

OPPOSITE, ABOVE Art Spiegelman and Françoise Mouly in one of the lofts of their SoHo apartment.

OPPOSITE, BELOW Much of the apartment—and library— is navigated via ladder.

all about the war between the sexes . . . very similar to James Thurber's stories, except the girls win most of the time. The characters are very convincing and believable, and the stories are simple, easy to track, and easy to understand."

Famous illustrators are also well represented: H. A. Rey of *Curious George,* Maurice Sendak of *Where the Wild Things Are,* and all of William Steig's work. "I should say," adds Mouly, "we do like chapter books, too!" And indeed, the shelves overflow with books in both French and English: existentialist philosophy, Kafka, Nabokov, Gertrude Stein, lots of history and noir. "I often feel we are drowning in our books," says Mouly. "How much more can we fit in? But how can we stop? This is what we do, how we live."

"They're nonnegotiable," says Spiegelman. "Comics help prepare you for the world."

ABOVE Art by friends—in some cases, applied directly to the wall—fills the home.

OPPOSITE, ABOVE LEFT Books—naturally—in Spiegelman's studio kitchen.

OPPOSITE, ABOVE RIGHT Art Spiegelman's studio.

OPPOSITE, BELOW A fiction shelf off the couple's dining room.

"WE DIDN'T HAVE DUPLICATE
COPIES, AND COULDN'T BEAR TO
GIVE UP THAT JOINT BOOKCASE!"

THE GUARDIANS

GAY & NAN TALESE
New York, New York

A SHARED LIBRARY, says Gay Talese, may have saved his marriage. "Back when we were first dating, we briefly broke up. But we had in common quite a few favorite writers: Graham Greene, Fitzgerald, of course, Cheever, Irwin Shaw" (who served as best man at the couple's wedding). "We didn't have duplicate copies, and couldn't bear to give up that joint bookcase!" The books, needless to say, have remained on the shelves of the East Side town house where the natty New Journalist and his equally legendary publisher-wife, Nan, have lived since 1957. And they have multiplied.

The town house comprises four book-filled floors and the basement study where Talese keeps famously well-organized notes on each of his own thirteen books and countless articles. (Currently, he's in the midst of an epic work about the couple's marriage.) The building's history is, to say the least, colorful: prior tenants included party girls, legendary directors, models, a blind dog, a famously dissipated harpist. The Taleses feel like perfect guardians of such a dramatic and entertaining history.

The house itself is elegant but lived in: impossibly high ceilinged, filled with art and photography by daughters Pamela and Catherine, and a good sprinkling of flowered chintz. The couple revamped the place in the early 1970s, and the silver-lacquered walls, mirrors, carpeting, and clean lines of the furniture evoke that era's glamour—without sacrificing comfort. It's easy to imagine both an abundance of entertaining and plenty of reading taking place within these walls.

On the first floor, many of the books are autographed by writers who've attended the Taleses' parties over the years: Lillian Hellman, Octavio Paz, Gabriel García Márquez. And in the case of regular author guests—Tom Wolfe, Gay's cousin Nick Pileggi—their oeuvres are given pride of place in the apartment's two front sitting rooms, near eye level. "The problem is, we have books quite literally in every room

OPPOSITE Just a few of the books that incited a marriage.

OVERLEAF, LEFT The house has played host to legendary parties. Many guests are represented on the bookshelves.

OVERLEAF, RIGHT Nan Talese, surrounded by the books she's edited and published.

of every floor," says Talese as he gestures around the living room, where carved built-in bookcases reach nearly to twenty-foot ceilings. "There's a *central* organizing principle," he says. "Nan's very good on that."

The trick, Nan says, is regular—and ruthless—purges. "I don't reread old books, there's too much to read, so in most cases we don't need them around." Where do they go? "It's wonderful," she says. "There's a man who takes them away. I think he sells what he can to the Strand and then donates the rest."

In the couple's comfortable bedroom, the floral-canopied bed faces an enormous bookcase. "These are all books I've edited," says Nan. "Not *all* the books I've edited, of course, that would be too many"—having worked at four publishing houses and, more recently, her eponymous Doubleday imprint—"but there's certainly a lot of Margaret Atwood in there, and Ian McEwan, Antonia Frasier, Pat Conroy. . . . And the lower bookshelf is Gay's books."

Nan also does all her reading on a white down sofa facing the bedroom fireplace, often in the company of dogs Bricker and Brontë. At the moment she's immersed in a novel called *Nine Continents*. Talese, for his part, does the bulk of his reading in his office area, sparsely decorated and filled with files and notes.

But as warned, the book collection spreads across the entire house: bookshelves on landings, in their daughters' bedrooms, which are now the guest rooms, and in a kitchenette. There are thousands of books. And there, in the dandy's capacious closet, among walls of meticulously kept hats and rows of bespoke shoes, are more bookshelves. "Books in the closet?" I say to him. He looks surprised. "Well, of course," he says.

"THE PROBLEM IS,
WE HAVE BOOKS
QUITE LITERALLY
IN EVERY ROOM
OF EVERY FLOOR."

ABOVE Gay Talese in his basement office.
LEFT Books in the closet? "Well, of course!"
OPPOSITE Books keep company with portraits
of the couple's daughters.

THE ART OF READING

THE ROYAL DANISH LIBRARY IS A STUDY in the happy cohabitation of old and new. While the original building has graced Copenhagen's waterfront for centuries, in 1999 architects Schmidt Hammer Lassen completed an extension known as the "Black Diamond" for its sharply angled walls and black granite cladding. Despite the name, the interior—centered around a large atrium—is light-filled and leads seamlessly into the vaulted halls of the original buildings. In addition to an auditorium, shop, café, and various exhibition locales, the new extension houses the library's art space. Modern artists are periodically commissioned with the task of arranging a piece on the rare books; the current installation (at the time of writing), Marina Abramović's "Method for Treasures," is centered around the viewer's experience of taking in some of the collection's rare books, including original Hans Christian Andersen manuscripts, letters by Søren Kierkegaard, and notations of Tycho Brahe.

ABOVE A study corner in the old portion of Copenhagen's Black Diamond.

OPPOSITE, ABOVE Treasures from the Danish National Library
are on rotating display.

OPPOSITE, BELOW The Black Diamond from Copenhagen harbor.

the PROFESSIONALS

A SHRINE TO TYPE

FRANCO MARIA RICCI
Parma, Italy

F RANCO MARIA RICCI LIVES IN HIS LIBRARY. "We built the house
around it," explains his wife, Laura Casalis. It is important to understand, however, that this is not the most eccentric thing about the art publisher's home,
which lies some thirty minutes outside of Parma's city center. After all, when one's
property involves an art museum, an inverted pyramid, the world's largest maze, a
classical doghouse, a ruin, and a Michelin-starred restaurant that incidentally grows
all its own produce and raises its own meat, well, living amid walls of antique books
begins to seem positively normal.

Ricci has never hewed to a conventional path. In a career that spans nearly seven
decades, he has become known not just for the bimonthly art magazine *FMR*—which
has been called "the most beautiful magazine in the world" and a showcase for luminaries like Calvino and Borges—but for his lavish Ricci Editore books, generally
printed in very limited editions, and characterized by such detail as handmade paper,
gold- and silver-embossed covers, and silk bindings.

The home/library (the couple eats in a separate structure several feet away),
remodeled from an outbuilding that belonged to Ricci's grandfather, contains all
his press's printed works. These range from a fully realized edition of Diderot and
d'Alembert's *Encyclopédie* to Luigi Serafini's *Codex Seraphinianus*, an encyclopedia of a whimsical alternate universe published in 1981. Reminiscent of a quixotic
eighteenth-century folly, this two-volume illustrated work is highly prized by collectors.

Ricci, who wears a signature flower in his buttonhole, is a typography obsessive
whose work has been influential in modern graphic design. As a teenager—then an
aspiring geologist—he first encountered the clean, distinctive typeface created by
Giambattista Bodoni, who in the eighteenth century served as the official printer to
the Duke of Parma. Bodoni has, ever since, been Ricci's signature font.

OPPOSITE This pyramid forms the centerpiece of Ricci's museum-cum-installation.

PREVIOUS PAGES Busts surround Ricci's collection of Boldoni books.

OVERLEAF The library, where Ricci treats his precious volumes like old friends.

Of the three large, barrel-vaulted rooms that compose the library, one is devoted entirely to two thousand of the works of Bodoni: the largest collection in the world. Many are the volumes specifically commissioned by the Duke of Parma's family, and they present an arresting contrast between the clean, seemingly modern type and the ornate, hand-inked lithograph illustrations. Ricci knows these books by heart, pulling the massive leather-bound folios down, flipping easily to pages he loves, touching the precious volumes with a combination of professional respect and almost familial affection. His nephew confirms this: "Since the age of three, he let me grow up around these books," he says. "I know them almost as well as he does."

Ricci shrugs. "I owe everything to Bodoni," he says simply.

While the rooms are impressive, certainly—decorated by a series of marble busts on plinths, and at one point, an effigy—there's a coziness to the scene. Part of this is due to Ricci's insouciance; he smokes small cigars with a seeming disregard for the fire hazard of eighteenth-century paper; the couple's two dogs, wirehaired Brigitte Bardot and suspicious Bamboo, run in and out of the building. Classical music plays softly. Ricci is especially fond, appropriately enough, of music from the baroque era.

Ricci, and his work, are deeply rooted in Parma. His family has lived in the region for centuries, and everything on his property—from the

"BOOKS WIN IN THE END."

Mannerist-filled museum, to the local cheeses and sparkling wine, to the busts of Parmesan dignitaries, to the library itself—is designed to showcase its riches. That he should live among the Bodonis, and the work Bodoni inspired, feels somehow apt.

Given his complete immersion in the world of books, it's perhaps no surprise that even Ricci's leisure reading is work related. "Depending on the project," he explains, "the bookshelf in my bedroom will have different things: history, or perhaps art history. . . . I immerse myself completely." He reads, only by day, at a small table by his bedroom window. Only occasionally does he read a modern novel; he does not follow trends in contemporary publishing and is generally underwhelmed by what he sees on the newsstand. "That is why I published everything," he explains, "because it was things I wanted to read." Good thing, then, that his own works make up such a large portion of the library. And yet, while no Luddite, he has an unwavering faith in the lure of print: He speaks not just of the tactile pleasures of paper, but also of the human love of possessing a physical object. "Books win in the end."

OPPOSITE, TOP LEFT Poplars line the drive between the museum and the house.

OPPOSITE, TOP RIGHT Franco Maria Ricci with his signature flower in his buttonhole.

OPPOSITE, BOTTOM LEFT The property has been in Ricci's family for generations.

OPPOSITE, BOTTOM RIGHT Ricci's collection of typography books is world-class.

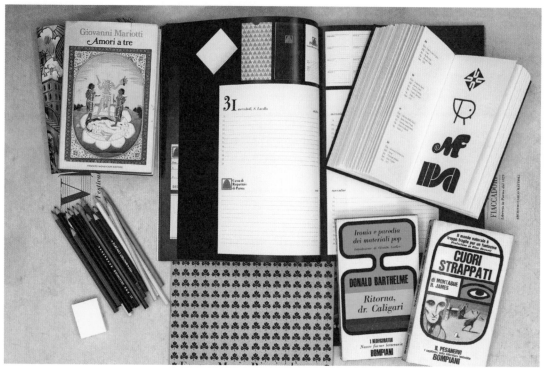

ABOVE LEFT The shelves have a library's organization.

ABOVE RIGHT A favorite Bodoni text. Ricci has used the typeface in much of his own work.

BELOW Ricci's worktable.

OPPOSITE A tribute to Ricci's hometown of Parma.

A LITERARY
RENAISSANCE

JAMES FENTON & DARRYL PINCKNEY
Harlem, New York

"OURS IS A WORKING LIBRARY," says the novelist and critic Darryl Pinckney, somewhat unnecessarily. It would be hard to overstate the scope of the accomplishments of Pinckney and his partner of twenty-five years, the poet, critic, and general intellectual polymath James Fenton. Whether the project in question is translating an operatic libretto (Fenton), completing a novel of 1960s black publishing (Pinckney), editing essays on Victorian interiors (Fenton), or considering the evolution of bebop (Pinckney), there are, at any given moment, a great many books in their collection to be consulted.

Indeed, the 1890 Harlem townhouse that the couple has been painstakingly restoring for the past eight years has some four dedicated libraries. Says Fenton, when they first visited the mansion, which was empty for eight years, "It was impossible to work out what certain parts had once been like." It had previously been a single room occupancy, a synagogue and school, and a clinic. There was graffiti on the walls, the basement held two or three inches of water, and the blocked drains had overflowed.

But it had been built as a grand family home by the baking soda magnate John Dwight, cofounder of Arm & Hammer, and behind the iron-spot Roman brick façade lay a stack of four oval rooms. The house had kept nearly all its original fireplaces and a great deal of its paneling and plasterwork. While it's still a work in progress, now the moldings shine, the parquet gleams, and the marble carving of the fireplaces is beautifully apparent. Walls are painted in rich, period-appropriate colors. Without living in a museum, they've managed to pay loving homage to the home's beauty. Fenton speaks of respecting "the general idiom of the original structure."

OPPOSITE The freshly revealed hall of the couple's brownstone.

As such, there are a series of lozenge-shaped libraries and accompanying, stained glass–bedecked reading nooks throughout the house: spots to make a bibliophile's heart skip a beat. A large parlor, containing two pianos and a working fireplace, tempts with deep couches and down armchairs. For more directed reading, however, each man also has a study where his own particular passions of the moment hold free rein. Says Pinckney, "My study houses American history, which means mostly black American history. For one year, in 1937, this house was the Harlem Community Art Center, and I sometimes think of Harlem Renaissance sculptress Augusta Savage walking its halls. Everything had been in boxes for the longest time, so to unpack and put books in some kind of usable order was actually a great leap forward, though the shelves look a mess."

There's also still plenty to be unpacked: Because the closets have no more room, twenty-five boxes of letters, manuscripts, galleys, and back issues sit against the walls, under the library table, and in the fireplace. "The movers brought them up four flights and here they have had to wait. These boxes make me feel that I am squatting in my own life. To open any of them would explode the past across the floor. Not all of this stuff comes from me, but James won't accept more boxes in his study, which is below mine and even more of a mess. Life with James means a lot of books."

Although Fenton's spare study is indeed filled with bookshelves and boxes, the vast majority of

ABOVE LEFT Darryl Pinckney and James Fenton at home.
ABOVE RIGHT The restoration is an ongoing work in progress.
OPPOSITE Organized chaos in the study.

his books are housed in a well-lit, far more contemporary space: a large, organized library fitted with minimalist Vitsoe shelving and halogen light fixtures. In another room, the wooden bookshelves were rescued—along with a great deal of stock—from a favorite bookshop. "We had no way of knowing that it would fit so perfectly," says Fenton—but indeed, the shelves could have been custom-built. "One of those happy coincidences."

The library is filled with poetry in French, Portuguese, Spanish—as well as translations and dictionaries. Each beloved poet has his own shelf. "One of my favorite English poets is George Herbert, and it happens that his *Complete English Works* is available in Everyman's Library, a handy hardback edited and introduced by Ann Pasternak Slater. This has modernized spelling, and nice clear print. And it has everything Herbert wrote in English, including his admirable collection of 'Outlandish Proverbs.'"

Of his own organizational systems, Pinckney says it's "nothing like James! I have things arranged chronologically, but there are also stacks on the tables, each a sad little memorial to a project I either don't have time for or don't make time to pursue. Everything in this room has too much meaning, down to the old coffee tin of political buttons and empty matchbooks. The table I use had been in the writer Elizabeth Hardwick's dining room. She did most of her typing on it. Even the books mean too much."

As to that once-waterlogged basement, it's now a library, too. "These are my gardening and landscaping books," explains Fenton of one entire room. "I brought them over from England. Eventually, the entire cellar will be given over to books. Well, quite like the rest of the house. And, indeed, our lives."

ABOVE Fenton bought the shelves from a favorite bookstore when it closed. "They fit almost miraculously," he says.

PREVIOUS PAGES The main library is a clean, modern contrast to the house's otherwise impeccable period authenticity.

OPPOSITE, ABOVE Books are stacked in every room.

OPPOSITE, BELOW An original stained glass window surrounded by Loeb classics.

"EVERY VOLUME IS CHOSEN FOR THE PLEASURE AND INTEREST OF THE CONTENTS, AND THE CONVENIENCE OF THE PRESENTATION."

A MAZE OF BOOKS

LIBRERÍA REGIA, IN MEXICO CITY'S DONCELES NEIGHBORHOOD, is a labyrinth of wonders. Lose yourself in the winding stacks of rare and used books, browsing, finding unexpected treasure, or just appreciating the sheer beauty of this downtown institution.

OPPOSITE This beloved Mexico City bookstore is a precarious labyrinth of volumes.

THE BUILDING BLOCKS
OF HOME

FERNANDA FRAGATEIRO & ANTÓNIO DE CAMPOS ROSADO
Lisbon, Portugal

"FOR ME, BOOKS ARE MATERIAL," says the artist Fernanda Fragateiro, whose sculptures and installations have frequently employed books. "People are shocked sometimes that I'll cut up a book. I wouldn't do it with a rare first edition." She indicates a sculpture in which a book has been deconstructed and covered in metal. "I saw a first edition of *Ulysses* at the Strand; I wouldn't use that! This is a 1970s German edition of *Ulysses*."

Fragateiro and her husband, António de Campos Rosado, live in Lisbon's old quarter in a beautiful nineteenth-century building; Fragateiro also has a studio several blocks away. The couple bought the building with friends many years ago and refurbished its woodwork, moldings, and Portuguese tiles. The apartment, incidentally, is where the Portuguese Communist Party was founded.

The book-lined study off the apartment's main room is a working library: art books, architecture, and poetry. Throughout a long and distinguished career de Campos Rosado has worked as a curator and director of public artworks. He says, "Art books are important partly because they come from museums, galleries, and exhibitions. Many were bought in those places. It's a unique form; with art sometimes a book is the only lasting thing. The art can be ephemeral. A show itself might be seen by thousands. But a book? Millions! The quality of the printing, the quality of the binding, it matters."

"I think German books smell the best," says Fragateiro. "Their construction and binding are very good."

Many of the books migrate between the apartment and Fragateiro's studio. "The books that are in regular use is one thing," she says. "Those will be on the table, they get moved more often." In this case, Fragateiro is studying Eileen Gray, On Kawara, and Anni and Josef Albers. "I'm reading these in a more fragmentary way,"

OPPOSITE A perfect reading nook—if you can crack the
bookshelves' idiosyncratic system.

181

she explains. "My reading is more like research." That said, she does read for what might be called pleasure, too, most recently, the Portuguese translation of *Isadora Duncan: A Life,* a gift from de Campos Rosado. "It's also about freedom, and a woman, so it makes sense for my work."

He adds, "We read for a purpose, usually. When I was younger, I read more for curiosity, not to *use* what I read. Now, I'll read books I'm not necessarily interested in. I want to know, but I'm not taking pleasure from them—it's work. And so I write, I underline, I use Post-its. It's not like a writer taking very thoughtful notes!"

"Most of our literature is in boxes," de Campos Rosado says. "All the books from my parents and childhood. We don't want to fill the place with books." Partially, he explains, this is in deference to Fragateiro's allergies; he wishes now that he'd built in sliding shelves to better protect the books from dust. "As it is, I have to vacuum and clean every few months. The cloth becomes black!"

The organizational methods are idiosyncratic. Says de Campos Rosado, "It's not alphabetical. I separated things into architecture, design, illustration. Then we have nature, science, traveling guides. Then within that, Portuguese and non-Portuguese. Within that, into books and monographs. Then recent, and less recent. And then, the books I use most"—these change quite a bit—"are more accessible, on their own shelves." One wall is devoted to references on the couple's own work, books he has edited and published: "a personal archive."

"Of course," adds Fragateiro, "a lot of books are missing because I use them in my sculpture. There's a whole missing library."

"THE ART CAN
BE EPHEMERAL.
A SHOW ITSELF
MIGHT BE SEEN
BY THOUSANDS.
BUT A BOOK?
MILLIONS!"

ABOVE A book becomes art.

OPPOSITE António de Campos Rosado and Fernanda Fragateiro in Lisbon.

182

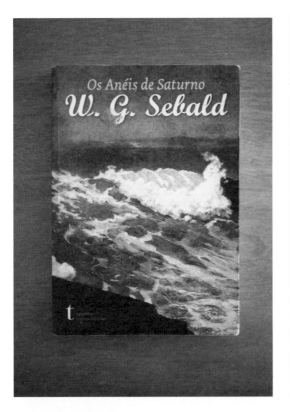

ABOVE LEFT A favorite Sebald title.

ABOVE RIGHT Books may be material to Fragateiro, but some are sacrosanct.

BELOW The couple values the beauty of books.

OPPOSITE The books are arranged alphabetically within categories . . . for the most part.

MAGICAL THINKING

"BOOKS ARE MAGIC" READS THE BRICK WALL outside the bookstore Emma Straub runs in Cobble Hill, Brooklyn. And despite having seen the business from both sides, as a bookseller and a best-selling author, Straub seems to have maintained faith in the credo. Straub had worked for many years at the nearby Book Court, and when that shop closed, she and her husband, Michael, decided to take up the baton. As she explains it, "You take the thing you love most in your neighborhood, and when it goes away you replace it." Of course, it was much more complicated than that, especially with two small children in the mix, but the result is a space of tremendous charm and character—known for not only its enchanting kids' nook but also its well-curated selection of new books.

"It is a third child, albeit one who sleeps through the night," says Straub, who concedes that owning Books Are Magic has altered her personal relationship to reading. "When it comes to my own reading," she says, "I feel bad that it's all so spoken-for in advance. I have a stack of books next to my bed that I want to read. I might get a chance in 2025, possibly." It's also altered the couple's approach to the books they own: They can, she says, edit more ruthlessly at home. And the order imposed by a bookstore carries over, too: "I've always been an alphabetizer—a shoddy one. But I do believe in it as an organizational principle."

ABOVE The wall of the building has already become a Brooklyn icon.

OPPOSITE A gathering place for the community where Straub draws on her experience as a novelist, a bookseller, and a reader.

A SPACE THAT LETS YOU
CATCH YOUR BREATH

SYLVIA BEACH WHITMAN
Paris, France

"MY DAD USED TO SAY, his two favorite moments of the day were opening the doors of the bookshop, with the excitement and wonder of who would come in that day," says Sylvia Beach Whitman. "And then closing the shop at night—he used to close at midnight—and take a book upstairs, like a miner that has struck treasure."

The bookshop in question is, of course, the legendary Left Bank literary mecca Shakespeare and Company; the dad, the equally legendary George Whitman, who ran the shop for some fifty years. Along the way he played host to most of the international literary world and a revolving cast of itinerant young people—"tumbleweeds" in S and Co. parlance.

Sylvia, named for the eponymous bookseller who originally founded Shakespeare and Company and was the publisher of *Ulysses,* has since her father's death been running the shop with her husband, striving to maintain the institution's character without falling into the complacency of cliché. She feels the shop can stand on the merits of literature, and that the book's demise has been greatly exaggerated. "I mean, people said when the *bicycle* was invented it was the end of the book—I think we've calmed down a bit about the death of the book."

It's a dance between concessions to modernity and fidelity to principle. They have added a café; taking photographs *is* still banned. "You feel it would be very easy to go the Disneyland route," she explains wryly. "T-shirts, and people dressed up like Hemingway for photos."

Sylvia Whitman has also made a conscious choice to maintain an autonomous existence: however inextricably she may be tied to Shakespeare and Company, she has an independent life, a separate apartment a few streets away—George lived above the shop—and a thriving private library quite independent of the store's inventory.

OPPOSITE Running a bookstore has taught Whitman to edit, but the shelves still overflow with the books she loves.

ABOVE French paperbacks in the kitchen.

OPPOSITE Whitman's work as a bookseller means she always has
multiple books on the go.

The first books she remembers receiving from her father were *The Hobbit, The Diary of a Young Girl,* and *Alice's Adventures in Wonderland*—stories, she points out, that combine escapism and political realities, and they have all remained comfort reads. "I remember his excitement about them, and his being really happy that I was going to go on those journeys." However, growing up in England, she did not come to really know her father—or the shop—until she was twenty-one.

For him, "the bookshop was his entire universe. Everything that existed outside those walls didn't exist for him." So she moved to Paris and learned the business. "There was no way to get to know one without the other; it was quite an odd experience, but it really made me fall in love with books, the bookshop, Paris, and him, all at once."

Walking into Whitman's apartment is indeed a different experience from being in the warren-like Shakespeare and Company: it's much lighter, for one thing, filled with pale wood, white-glazed pottery, and open, pine bookshelves. ("Normally with shelves I'm so used to getting them built, so it was fun buying something already made.")

Despite the presence of a small son, clutter is at a minimum: it's a space that lets you catch your breath.

Because she is surrounded by such literary bounty during working hours, Whitman has edited her personal collection to only those books she truly loves: a fabulously lurid 1970s edition of *Rebecca; Brooklyn Follies;* poetry by Walt Whitman and Emily Dickinson; *The End of the Affair*—the first book she ever gave her husband—a first British edition of *Tender Is the Night*. One of Whitman's passions is fairy tales:

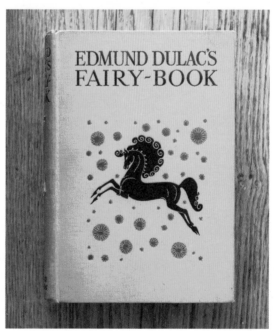

ABOVE A first UK edition of a favorite book.

BELOW Whitman has collected fairy tales for many years.

OPPOSITE Books are arranged by subject, then author.

illustrated Edmund Dulac, Italo Calvino's folk-tales, Angela Carter's reimagined feminist fables. She recently did a major culling. "It was getting to be too much; like my dad, I'd take a book every day from the bookshop, and they were piling up. There's often that feeling that I can't resist taking it back, even though I know I won't have time to read it."

While she doesn't consider herself a serious collector of early editions, Whitman says her time working in Shakespeare and Company's rare book room gave her an appreciation for precious books' idiosyncrasies. "Talk about the beauty of the object! But it's also that each edition has a story—where you'll know that with, say, a true first they forgot to print the name of the photographer of the author photo on the back, or there was some terrible mistake made on the title page—I like that history of the printing, on top of the story of the actual book."

Her first editions are "quite mixed in" with the other hundreds of books, all of which are alphabetized by author's last name. "I've gone from being really chaotic and having piles everywhere to something more conventional. It's a bit more boring than some filing systems like 'interesting marriages,' but much easier to find. And I do go back to books so much—they're a real reference in my life—I like to be able to find them, underline in pencil, and annotate. So often with books, I feel as though they're filled with the answers to questions: questions about yourself, the world. So I want to be able to find them when I need them."

She reads constantly—both for events at the shop, and because the tempting array of new titles flooding the shop, in both French and English, is simply too strong a lure to resist. She says she

"I LIKE THE HISTORY OF THE PRINTING, ON TOP OF THE STORY OF THE ACTUAL BOOK."

has "had to become quite ruthless"—she stops reading a book she doesn't like after fifty pages. "There's never a moment where I don't have the next thing in mind; often it evolves around the events in the bookshop—having the privilege of meeting these authors, I do want to make the most of it. And, of course, as a bookseller one must keep up with the literary prizes. Now that Tom Wolfe's dead, I'm going to finally read *Bonfire of the Vanities*, which I've always meant to." As she is expecting a baby, she's now devouring works on mothers; she highly recommends Sheila Heti's *Motherhood*. She manages to get through several in a typical week. "If I were really logical, I'd have a system: I'd read one in English, one in French, one classic, one contemporary . . . but of course that's never how it is!"

She does all her reading at home, stretched out on a deep sofa set under a window, as soon as she wakes up. "Reading in the morning is a totally different mode to the evening. I remember one morning, the sun was pouring in and I just read, in one stretch, *The Year of Magical Thinking*. It was one of these moments of perfection—I mean, I was sobbing, obviously—but the silence, the light; I feel like you're praying, just slightly differently."

OPPOSITE Sylvia Beach Whitman in the rare book room of Shakespeare and Company.

OVERLEAF Whitman loves to read first thing in the morning, before the house is stirring.

"SO OFTEN WITH BOOKS, I FEEL AS THOUGH THEY'RE FILLED WITH THE ANSWERS TO QUESTIONS: QUESTIONS ABOUT YOURSELF, THE WORLD. SO I WANT TO BE ABLE TO FIND THEM WHEN I NEED THEM."

THE BIBLIOPHILE'S
LAIR

MICHAEL SILVERBLATT

Los Angeles, California

"I'VE ALWAYS SORT OF DREADED KNOWING the exact number," says Michael Silverblatt of his library. "I couldn't even begin to guess; it's in the tens of thousands. Those of us who are readers, I find, are rarely counters."

Silverblatt is one of the great readers. As host of the legendary radio program The Bookworm, he has been interviewing writers for decades, with a thoroughness and knowledge that has gained him both a devoted following and a massive library. This is largely because, prior to his interviews, Silverblatt makes a point of reading an author's entire oeuvre; he'll also keep any first novels he finds promising in the hopes that the author will write more. "I like to have a library full of the books I love, so that if I think of a passage from Proust or Barthelme, old or new, I can go down and find it."

"I'm lucky enough to have one apartment for my life, and another for my books," he explains. The apartment intended for people, which is comfortable and orderly, is also extremely book friendly—as is every space he occupies. But while Silverblatt may venerate the written word, he's not precious about his library: The shelves are a combination of bespoke and IKEA; the editions are everything from first to paperbacks he's picked up to give friends. He loves owning multiples of his favorites. "If I meet someone who's a sensitive reader, they need to own Randall Jarrell's anthology of stories," he explains. "Eventually you do have to send some into the world, but I'll tell you the truth, it's very difficult. Very. Duplicates and triplicates are the first

"THOSE OF US WHO ARE READERS, I FIND, ARE RARELY COUNTERS."

OPPOSITE Michael Silverblatt has "always sort of dreaded" knowing just how many books he owns.

199

to go. Like many people, I can't feel I ever really *own* a book."

The books are alphabetized by author, with sections for anthologies, fairy tales, and myth, but Silverblatt's knowledge of the library goes beyond mere organization. Although he denies having a photographic memory, he admits that "when I'm looking for a line I've read, I tend to remember the place on the page, its relationship to the rest of the text. The books I read are like real experiences, and as such they imprint like any life experience of great intensity."

Silverblatt doesn't drive, which is unusual for a denizen of Los Angeles—"I'm a real New Yorker that way"—and so getting to the city's bookstores isn't an easy matter. "Whenever I was depressed," he says, "I used to go walking around a bookstore. Now, I can go downstairs, and it's like the best used bookstore ever. All the books I love."

ABOVE Michael Silverblatt, among his books, in Los Angeles.

OPPOSITE, ABOVE Silverblatt has "one apartment for life, and one for books."

OPPOSITE, BELOW LEFT A book Silverblatt wants every sensitive reader to experience.

OPPOSITE, BELOW RIGHT A desert-island read.

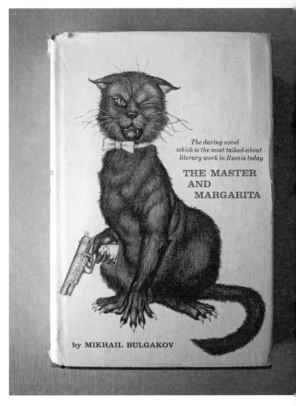

ANN PATCHETT

"I'M NOT SURE BOOKSELLING HAS INFORMED my relationship with books as much as age has," says Ann Patchett, who, as a novelist and proprietor of Nashville's Parnassus, spends her life among books. Of her home library she says, "I have to keep them moving in and moving out. I've never been sentimental. The only books I really care about as objects are the ones in which my parents wrote me birthday notes. The books I love the most are the ones I never have because I've passed them on to someone else, so I just buy a few more copies to have on hand." Of the great volumes she's sent, Patchett says, "So many books arrive at the house I have to be fiercely honest with myself all the time: If I'm never going to read it, it has to go. My office is a temporary station for books I'm reading or thinking about reading. If I decide to keep a book, I shelf it alphabetically in the library downstairs."

ABOVE Parnassus Books is a Nashville must-visit for readers.

OPPOSITE Ann Patchett and co-owner Karen Hayes at Parnassus.

READING
BY DESIGN

CORALIE BICKFORD-SMITH
London, England

WHEN CORALIE BICKFORD-SMITH WAS ASKED to design a self-portrait for a magazine feature, it consisted of the following text, superimposed over a large pair of spectacles: "There's more to life than books, you know. But not much more." It's a philosophy that's immediately apparent in the colorful three-story house the award-winning artist and designer shares with her husband on the outskirts of London. The visitor is greeted with a bookcase containing some of the myriad books Bickford-Smith has designed, which are as varied and imaginative as the texts themselves.

Bickford-Smith has designed any number of iconic series—and covers—in her fifteen years at Penguin Books. But perhaps her most familiar works are the Clothbound Classics: limited editions of the literary canon, each cover distinct in its coloration and embossed patterns. These have spawned an almost cultish following; if someone manages to acquire them all, they'll have achieved not just a complete library of English literature classics, but also a strikingly lovely one.

"I wanted to create books that could be passed down through generations," she explains of her initial impetus. "And I was obsessed with William Morris, beautiful Arts and Crafts cloth binding." She lobbied to do a clothbound hardcover of Hans Christian Andersen fairy tales—"People were a bit 'What are you doing?'"—but the claret-colored volume, embossed with designs from Andersen's own paper cutouts, proved so popular that she was quickly given the task of designing ten more in three weeks. In designing the covers, "I read the book, research textiles of the era," and mine details of the text to find sometimes hidden decorative motifs, such as a

"I WANTED TO CREATE BOOKS THAT COULD BE PASSED DOWN THROUGH GENERATIONS."

OPPOSITE Visitors are greeted, sort of, by books that Bickford-Smith has designed.

flower or a detail that might otherwise escape the eye of the reader.

Together on a low shelf in the living room, the accumulated classics make a beautiful display. Bickford-Smith is modest about her work. "I'm too busy working to think too much about how they're amazing—I try not to be precious about them," she says. But she admits to a few favorites: the gray, black-embossed *Dracula* is one. "Because the colors are so limited. And the garlic flowers"—a stylized Art Nouveau-ish floral—"keep Dracula locked away by your bedside." She's also fond of *Don Quixote*. "He went mad from reading all the books. But I wanted to do him as he saw himself: a classic knight in shining armor." The suits of armor are rendered in gold on a tangerine field.

She is currently finishing her third book, and at home Bickford-Smith works in a cozy study on the top floor filled with light, books, and topography, her original area of study. "I thought the third would be a bit easier, but it's not. I'm exploring what a jungle looks like, so I can inhabit a visual world. It's a sort of mental battle, trying to get what's in my head out onto the page. But when it's rolling, it's the best."

For pleasure, she reads before bed: favorite titles include Murakami's memoir *What I Talk About When I Talk About Running,* and Emilie Pine's essays, *Notes to Self*—"the most brutal, honest, beautiful book." At the time we met, she was midway through Elif Batuman's *The Idiot.* When asked if she ever uses an electronic reader, she replied, "I have to have the physical book, because I need to know how many pages I've got, I need a map," she says. And of keeping old volumes: "I love physical books, because you find all these memories—bookmarks, turned-down pages, notes. It's like having a little document of that moment in time. A bit of autobiography."

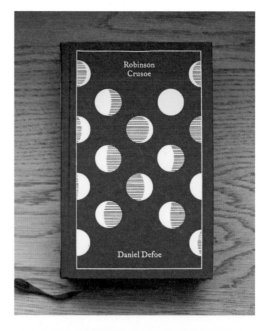

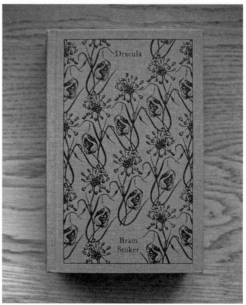

PREVIOUS PAGES The Penguin clothbound classics have developed an obsessive following.

TOP *Robinson Crusoe* is embellished with the phases of the moon.

OPPOSITE, TOP LEFT Coralie Bickford-Smith at home in London.

OPPOSITE, TOP RIGHT A corner of the top-floor studio.

WHERE BOOKS HAVE
THEIR OWN FLOOR

LEE & WHITNEY KAPLAN
Los Angeles, California

"I PERSONALLY HAVE ALWAYS BEEN a glass-half-empty sort of person," says Lee Kaplan. "But I absolutely do still love books. There's a dichotomy between loving the books and the way the business has headed. My solace is really the object." He's talking about the bookstore business, an undoubted challenge in the era of the Internet. Yet, to book lovers, Kaplan's Arcana: Books on the Arts remains the standard, and its proprietor is a living legend.

Kaplan's first job was cataloging his grandfather's vast library; later he worked in an L.A. bookstore, and in 1984 he opened Arcana in a one-bedroom apartment in Westwood. Since 2012, Arcana (which is co-owned by Lee's wife, Whitney) has occupied the Helms Bakery building in Culver City. Although Kaplan is known as something of a savant in his field, he gives equal credit to his loyal customer base. "Ours is a very specialist store, but traditionally ours was a clientele that didn't need to be led." He describes Arcana as "a sanctuary." As he says, matter-of-factly, "I know how completely insane and inefficient this business is; no one interested in the bottom line would have taken the route I did, or failed to change it in the past ten years."

Recently, the couple moved to a light-filled, breathable two-level home nearby. And their home library is, well, massive. "I've had the luxury of having a bookstore for thirty-five years and buying wholesale, so we have a very, very sprawling book collection that's in no sense edited," says Kaplan. "And frankly, it's caused problems with how we live." It's only because of the new duplex that things have changed in the past year. "One for us—quite

> "WE HAVE A VERY, VERY SPRAWLING BOOK COLLECTION THAT'S IN NO SENSE EDITED."

OPPOSITE A shelf at the legendary Arcana showing books on the arts.

211

spare—and one for the library. It's the first time in probably fifteen years we've actually been able to have people over; before, there were just too many books."

Though the Kaplans can technically off-load their excess books to the store, "There's no room on the shelves there either! That said, if a book is really precious, I'll often transfer it to the shop; I can live with a reprint." Of the stock—used, new, rare, and specialized—one thing is true: "We won't just sell you good books, we'll sell you great books."

ABOVE Lee and Whitney Kaplan in Los Angeles.

OPPOSITE, ABOVE Lee and Whitney's personal collection at their new duplex; the boxes neatly filed to be unpacked.

OPPOSITE, BELOW Many Angelenos credit Kaplan with curating their informal art education.

A TRIBUTE TO LOCAL
CREATIVITY
(AND CHOCOLATE)

CASA BOSQUES IS A HAPPY, colorful independent bookstore in Mexico City's vibrant neighborhood of Colonia Roma Norte. The white-painted shop has a deep selection of foreign magazines and art and design books, making this a tribute to local creativity. It's also perhaps the only bookshop in the world with its own line of chocolates, flavored with local flavors like rosemary, chile pasillo, and sea salt.

ABOVE The shop's director, artist Jorge de la Garza.

OPPOSITE Unique bookshelf display.

A HAPPY MIX

WHILE THE WORD "CURATION" IS USED a lot these days, Copenhagen's Cinnober reminds you of the value of a discerning eye and a strong point of view. The bookshop, near the city's Round Tower, was founded by Ulla Welinder, a graphic designer, and Morten Voigt, an illustrator, so it's no surprise that it's visually arresting and considered. Along with a careful selection of books on art, photography, graphic and industrial design, architecture, and photography, Cinnober carries beautiful paper goods and stationery and a changing selection of designed art and objects. The airy, welcoming space also hosts exhibitions and events; it's truly a design hub.

OPPOSITE Each book and object for sale at Cinnober is carefully selected for display.

the COLLECTORS

THE GRAND ACQUISITOR

MICHAEL BOYD
Los Angeles, California

"W HEN I WAS A KID, my parents were academics," says Michael Boyd, "and I remember one of their colleagues had a book: *The Syrian Wine Trade 1845–1860*. I just thought, wow. That title, in its specificity, just seemed to me simultaneously aspirational, inspirational, lofty, and practical." As such, he now takes pleasure in applying similar concision to his own interests. When asked what the focus of his library is, he responds without missing a beat: "Modernism, architecture, design, and art from 1900 to 1970."

Growing up in Berkeley, Boyd says these interests didn't impress his parents. "My dad called them my picture books. But then he was a structural linguist." When Boyd started his own studies, "I was a freshman and went to the bookstore to get my textbooks. I got distracted and spent all my money on Noguchi."

His interests would ultimately pay off: Boyd is now renowned not just as a designer, but also as a collector, architectural restorer, and authority on modernism. He and his wife live in Oscar Niemeyer's Strick House in Santa Monica, the architect's sole residential property in the United States. The house in turn is filled with treasures: pieces by Charles Eames, Carlo Mollino, and Jean Prouvé, showcased by the house's fourteen-foot-high glass walls.

Boyd's library, meanwhile, numbers some ten thousand books, organized by field and topic—"say, an architectural movement"—and then alphabetically. "I can put my hands on anything; people are amazed. It's a brain type." The same is presumably true of Boyd's vast collection of vintage guitars, which shares space with the books; in a previous life, Boyd worked as a composer.

Boyd is *not* a book lender. "I have lent books out and had exclusively bad experiences," he says. "There has been loss and damage." He's particularly sensitive to

OPPOSITE A few of Michael Boyd's consuming obsessions, Los Angeles.

221

this. "One of my hobbies is paper restoration, so every jacket is in mint condition. I'm fanatical about condition."

However, he and his wife are willing to sell their things, if only to maintain the space for new interests. "I've got to be one of the most acquisitive beings—in the ninety-ninth percentile at least—although everything is used. People are horrified that we have auctions. But that allows me to keep looking and picking and shopping. I let the titles wash over me, and I think about whether I really still need something in my life. I can be absolutely done with an artist or architect. I take the lessons from them, but it's no longer relevant to my work." In conclusion? "The older I get, the more I care about the essence."

"I WAS A FRESHMAN AND WENT TO THE BOOKSTORE TO GET MY TEXTBOOKS. I GOT DISTRACTED AND SPENT ALL MY MONEY ON NOGUCHI."

BELOW Restoring the Oscar Neimeyer house was a labor of love.

OPPOSITE PAGE Boyd is punctilious about regularly culling his library.

OVERLEAF The collection is rigorously organized and cataloged.

"ONE OF MY HOBBIES
IS PAPER RESTORATION,
SO EVERY JACKET IS
IN MINT CONDITION.
I'M FANATICAL ABOUT
CONDITION."

"IN THE PAST WE
USED TO READ
TOGETHER.
BUT NOW, WITH
THE KIDS, IT'S
MUCH MORE TOMI
UNGERER BOOKS!"

A COLLECTOR'S EYE,
A READER'S HEART

MICHAEL FUCHS & CONSTANCE BRETON
Berlin, Germany

"IT'S LIKE AN ADDICTION," says Michael Fuchs of his book habit. "You have to maintain it; you're constantly in a state of struggle. You build another space for books, and suddenly that's full, too, and you're back in the same place."

Gallerist Fuchs has been collecting art books and monographs for the better part of thirty years, and the resulting library makes an impression upon entering the Berlin apartment he shares with his wife, art consultant Constance Breton, and their two children. Of course, the entire experience is somewhat arresting: The family lives in a building called Mädchenschule, a 1930s Jewish girls' school in the Mitte neighborhood. Long abandoned, the building's fourteen classrooms, sports hall, and a rooftop playground are now a multiuse arts space; the couple lives on one floor.

The building combines institutional bones (the architect was a proponent of the functional Neue Sachlichkeit—or New Objectivity—style) and an artistic vibrancy. As to the expansive, meandering apartment, it's serene without feeling cold. The furnishings are beautiful and include a Jean Prouvé desk, Ingo Maurer chairs, Verner Panton rugs, a Serge Mouille lamp. And the space manages to be inviting, providing plenty of room for small children. Narrow bookcases divide the rooms.

Fuchs's vast collection is, naturally, heavy on art and design, with an emphasis on modernism and forays into everything from Albrecht Dürer to Edward Hopper. Books and monographs are both alphabetized. For pleasure, he still tends to read to a purpose; when we spoke he was reading Luc Boltanski and Arnaud Esquerre's *The Economic Life of Things,* an analysis of consumer goods.

"My books are much more personal," says Breton. "I'm as messy as he is tidy. They pile up. It's very hard for me to throw things away; I move with my books." Her tastes are also more catholic; lately she has been absorbed in Elena Ferrante's

OVERLEAF Books are shelved by subject, and auction catalogs have their own section.

Neapolitan Quartet and Heidi Chiavaroli's *The Hidden Side*.

"In the past," she remembers, "we used to read together. But now, with the kids, it's much more Tomi Ungerer books!" And while they hope one day their children will inherit their library, for the moment their young son is fixated on a single volume: "He always goes to a Christie's catalog from the Aga Khan's jewelry sale in Geneva, 1988. Well, it's bright green."

But on vacation, the couple plans to read seriously. "It will be a book every two days. The new Murakami; this biography of Picasso I've been wanting to read. No picture books allowed."

ABOVE LEFT The unique building was originally a Jewish girls' school.

ABOVE RIGHT Constance Breton and Michael Fuchs.

A BIG PASSION FOR
TINY BOOKS

"PEOPLE HAVE ASKED ME, WHY TINY BOOKS?" says Neale Albert. "I say, 'What else fits in New York?'" Of course, when the miniature books in question number more than 4,500, that's still a good amount of real estate; the bulk of the attorney's collection lives in its own "cottage" on the second floor of the apartment Albert shares with his wife, Margaret.

Albert, a two-time president of the Miniature Book Society, is a big collector of little things. On a trip to England years ago, he stopped in to a miniatures show on a whim and was immediately captivated by the artistry on display. Scale models of actual pubs and Palladian villas gave birth to a tiny library building, which in turn became a fascination with the six-point-type books that were needed to fill its shelves. "What do you need for a library? Books!" he explains, so he began hitting the minibook dealers. From collecting it was a small step to publishing, and the rest is miniatures legend.

While Albert has plenty of minute books that are notable purely for their exquisite execution—full sets of Shakespeare that require the use of a magnify-

ABOVE A tiny part of an important (and tiny) collection.

232

ing glass, for instance, and an infinitesimal Chekhov story that *may* be the smallest book in the world—his true passion is for more idiosyncratic commissions. A small, perfectly accurate globe holds a nineteenth-century *Atlas of the British Empire*. A box containing a hidden key unlocks a tiny volume of erotica by the photographer Max Vadukul. "I like to say to artists, 'What's the hardest thing you ever did?' And then I ask them to top it," he says. However, he gives the craftspeople—leatherworkers, papermakers, artists—tremendous latitude after that. The commissions routinely take years to complete. He regards a case filled with tiny, exquisite books of hand-marbled paper. "I feel like I'm the father to each of these books," he says.

Albert's work has been displayed at the Grolier Club, a New York mecca for bibliophiles and he has a philosophical take on what it means to collect. "Collecting is not about owning things," says Albert. "It's about finding things and meeting people. You don't need to own to be a collector."

ABOVE Much of the print requires a magnifying glass to read.

A TWO-STORY LIBRARY
INSPIRES AND INFORMS

PEDRO REYES & CARLA FERNANDEZ
Mexico City, Mexico

T HE POURED-CONCRETE HOUSE that artist Pedro Reyes shares with his wife, designer Carla Fernandez, and their two children in Mexico City is part experimental artists' compound, part political statement, part sculpture, and, in large part, a library. Built partially of handmade cement bricks, and leavened in spots with bright pops of color, the house is simultaneously menacing and cozy, rooted in both the Mexican folk tradition and brutalist modernism. Like the artist himself, it resists easy characterization.

While known for politically engaged, large-scale projects, Reyes has worked in almost every medium one can think of—most recently, political puppet theater. However, there are through lines in his work, passions he shares with Fernandez: activism, Mexican artistic heritage, and a profound love of books.

A two-story library forms the literal center of the house. Although it's enormous—easily as large as many public libraries—Reyes says his bibliophilic appetites are more than equal to the task of filling it. Not only has he been collecting and retaining books since childhood, but "I probably buy two hundred to three hundred books a month," he also confesses. "On every trip, I come back with three suitcases of books." And he travels extensively.

The library, he says, is the center of both family life and the couple's extensive social life; their home is a popular meeting place for their artistic and political circle. "It's meant for both work and leisure," he says. "Most of our conversations here revolve around books; we spend a lot of time taking them out and then rearranging the collection."

Although he cannot hope to keep up with his intake, Reyes reads extensively and is a font of recommendations. He loves Milton Erickson's *My Voice Will Go with You*. "I only get rid of 0.5 percent of my books. I regret when I lend a book, because it always happens that at some point, you need it. On some few occasions, I buy two copies if there is a book I would like to share."

OPPOSITE The two-story library is built from poured concrete.

235

ABOVE The library's atrium opens onto greenery.

OPPOSITE Carla Fernandez and Pedro Reyes.

236

"I PROBABLY BUY
TWO HUNDRED TO
THREE HUNDRED BOOKS
A MONTH. ON EVERY
TRIP, I COME BACK
WITH THREE SUITCASES
OF BOOKS."

Politically engaged, Reyes reads extensively on current events and our relationship with technology. His recent puppet show, which was originally based on Noam Chomsky's *Manufacturing Consent*, featured characters based on Steve Jobs, Donald Trump, and Elon Musk literally printing the authors of their choosing from a machine—in their case, Ayn Rand. Justin Peters's *The Idealist* has also been a recent inspiration.

However, as the scale of the library would indicate, Reyes is something of a literary omnivore; other favorites include Paul Goodman's *Growing Up Absurd, The Marriage of Cadmus and Harmony* by Roberto Calasso, and the selected writings of Charles Fourier. The unifying theme, he says, is a simple one: "Books are the only object where the dilemma between having and being is cancelled, as the more books you have, the more resourceful you become."

ABOVE, LEFT The library forms the center of the house.

ABOVE, RIGHT Indoors meets outdoors.

OPPOSITE The house celebrates traditional Mexican art and craftsmanship.

THE SECRET BOOKSTORE

BRAZENHEAD BOOKS, THE SPEAKEASY BOOKSTORE run out of a private apartment in an undisclosed location, is almost an urban legend in New York. But as invited guests know, Michael Seidenberg's hidden gem is very real. After rising rents sent his shop out of business, the proprietor went underground, so to speak, carting the thousands of books into his Upper East Side apartment. When zoning officials closed that operation down, he moved again, slightly downtown; the address is provided on a strictly need-to-know basis. The space, crowded with heavy bookshelves and stacks of volumes, is home to periodic readings and literary events as well as the bookseller himself, who lives on the premises.

ABOVE Michael Seidenberg, proprietor, who passed away in July 2019

OPPOSITE Before its closing in 2019, the address was provided on a need-to-know basis.

FOOD FOR THOUGHT

CAROLINE RANDALL WILLIAMS

Nashville, Tennessee

"WE ALWAYS SAY IN MY FAMILY that we've known from the beginning that food and words go together," says the Nashville-based Caroline Randall Williams. To the poet, academic, and author, her collection of cookbooks is more than reference—it's a cultural history. "It is a *living* collection. It is part of my inheritance and my legacy; it is part of the foundations of not only who I am in abstract ways but also what my home is in elemental, spatial ways. I go to it all the time. I am still learning it. I love looking at it and engaging with it. I think and write about it as a collective artifact, and I peruse it for inspiration from individual books."

Williams, who coauthored 2015's *Soul Food Love* with her mother, author Alice Randall, cannot separate the collection from her family. "My grandmother began it as a young, newly married woman in Nashville. Or really, maybe, it started before she married my grandfather—there are a couple of books where she's written Joan Bontemps in the front, which was her maiden name. She was a librarian and the daughter of a brilliant home cook and a Harlem Renaissance poet. . . . I love knowing that the collecting grew as she fed people from the home she built with my grandfather, who was a civil rights lawyer in Nashville. These were the books that inspired her as she welcomed people fighting for freedom to her table."

The collection now numbers hundreds of volumes—new, old, community cookbooks, and pamphlets; Maya Angelou's *Hallelujah! The Welcome Table,* and *The Jewish Japanese Sex and Cook Book* ("a source of intrigue for me since I was a girl")—making it hard to narrow down the most influential. "If I had to identify a single formative volume, I would have to say the early 1940s edition of then *Ebony* magazine food editor Freda DeKnight's *Date with a Dish.* It was a cookbook by black women for black women, written in the spirit of cooking for celebration and for comfort and for quality in their own homes, which was a revelation at the time and continues to be a triumph to me." While the organizational methods may

OPPOSITE Three generations' worth of cookbook collecting.

243

be opaque to the outside viewer, "After so many years of living with the books, I have my own sense of where everything is. If you wanted to get your hands on *Dinner at Buckingham Palace* or *Feasts for All Seasons* or *A Taste of Country Cooking* I would know almost exactly where on the shelves to go. So there's method, but the method is mostly my madness at this point." And it's not diminishing anytime soon: "I really don't edit at this point—part of the joy of the collection is its ranginess, its breadth, its depth, its eccentricity."

When pushed, however, she will admit to one particularly meaningful volume. "If the house were burning, I'd probably rush to save *The New World Encyclopedia of Cooking*, purely because Nana pressed fresh flowers into its pages, and I would be heartbroken if I failed to preserve them."

ABOVE Caroline Randall Williams in Nashville.

OPPOSITE, ABOVE LEFT Handwritten notes provide snatches of biography.

OPPOSITE, ABOVE RIGHT A collection in constant use.

OPPOSITE, BELOW Some books are rarities, some are novelties, but all are beloved.

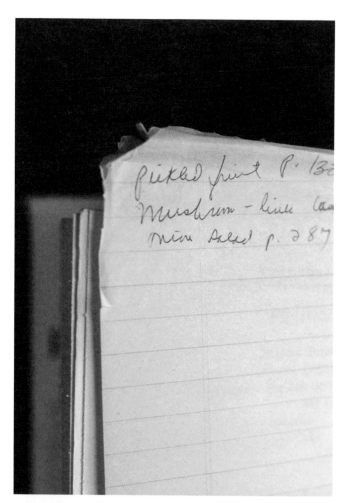

COOKBOOKS FOR COLLECTORS

"PEOPLE WILL ALWAYS EAT, and they'll always read," says Bonnie Slotnick, whose eponymously named antiquarian cookbook shop in New York's East Village—recently relocated after losing its lease—is a heartening story of survival. Indeed, even as other specialty bookstores have closed their doors, the cookbook shop has proved resilient. In New York, Nach Waxman's Upper East Side stalwart Kitchen Arts & Letters, London's legendary Books for Cooks, and San Francisco's Omnivore all provide a mix of events, classes, and (in the case of Books for Cooks) food—whether you're interested in actual cooking manuals or the pleasures of an armchair read.

ABOVE Generations' worth of instruction.

OPPOSITE A beacon for cookbook mavens in the East Village.

TRAVELING
THE WORLD IN A PARISIAN
APARTMENT

CAROLINA IRVING
Paris, France

"E VEN WHEN I'M READING, here at home, it's about travel," says Carolina Irving. Born in New York to Venezuelan parents, Irving has lived between France and Portugal since she was a teenager and spends a large portion of her year working in Asia, Africa, and other parts of Europe. A student of seventeenth-century Italian art history and archaeology who creates vibrant, globally inspired textiles in her Grands Boulevards apartment, the elegant Irving's ruling passions are visible everywhere.

The first thing that strikes the visitor is the color in her Parisian home: faded peony-pink velvet, blue-striped woven carpet, antique-sari lamp shades, wine-colored tribal embroideries from Afghanistan, and brightly flowered pillows from Morocco, all as varied in texture as in shade. Like the potpourri that scents the air, the effect is not dizzying or excessive; rather it feels personal and warm. This mixture of weaves, patterns, and colors is not merely Irving's signature; it's what she loves—the history and culture of each piece, the handiwork that distinguishes one textile from another. "I love that people have handled them, that they have history," she explains. "That makes them easy to live with."

Through a set of French doors, one looks directly onto the tall bookshelves that line the dining room. Indeed, there are books everywhere: in stacks in the jade-green bedroom, on low tables, in a niche by the marble fireplace. Like so much else about the home, the book collection is a combination of travelogue and research library. Art history, textile history, catalogs from exhibitions and auctions, historical tracts, memoirs of Marco Polo and Herodotus—the collection, which is sorted by subject, is vast and dynamic. Irving says she is forever pulling down a volume for inspiration, to see what sparks a thought or to find a half-remembered image. There's even a rolling ladder for that purpose.

OPPOSITE An antique rosary and a wooden mushroom
flank travel books.

249

The shelves were custom-built for her collection, but, as she explains, she is forever overflowing them: "I travel, and I become fascinated with the batiks of Indonesia, or a Japanese indigo that is new to me—a new obsession is born, and I want to know everything about it! I also have a bad habit of buying books wherever I go."

The books themselves create a colorful cacophony on the shelves, a warm natural wallpaper interspersed with snapshots of Irving's family, bits of pottery and sculpture. It's unstudied and serious at once. Irving is a designer, with a trained eye—but this is no decorative collection. Like everything about the apartment, it is lived in, well loved, and imprinted with that overused word *authenticity*. The home is also arranged for optimal reading comfort, with good lighting over down-filled chairs, silk-covered swinging lamps mounted by the bed, and convenient stacks of books close to hand from every seat in the apartment.

A voracious reader, Irving devours new fiction: Zadie Smith, Jhumpa Lahiri, Han Kang. "There aren't enough hours in the day—in a life!" Her comfort books, however, are all to do with travel and discovery: T. E. Lawrence's sweeping memoirs, Lawrence Durrell's *Bitter Lemons of Cypress*, Bruce Chatwin's *In Patagonia,* the personal travelogues of "Patrick Leigh Fermor, the pioneering Freya Stark. You know: the classics!"

"Whatever I read," she says, "is a reminder of places I have been, or of where I'd like to go. Adventures—even tame ones. For me, it is a combination of work and pleasure. But then, life should be like that!"

ABOVE Carolina Irving in Paris.

BELOW Treasures collected on Irving's travels.

OPPOSITE Varied textiles and a rose sofa make this a perfect reading spot.

"WHATEVER I READ
IS A REMINDER
OF PLACES I HAVE
BEEN, OR OF WHERE
I'D LIKE TO GO.
ADVENTURES—
EVEN TAME ONES."

ABOVE Travel and art books piled high in the dining room.

OPPOSITE, ABOVE A glimpse of the purpose-built bookshelves from the entryway.

OPPOSITE, BELOW In the living room, comfort and color are the unifying themes.

OVERLEAF The library-dining room . . . or is it the other way around?

THE CABINET
OF CURIOSITIES

PRINCE LOUIS ALBERT DE BROGLIE

Paris, France, and Lisbon, Portugal

"I 'M A PERSON WHO ACTS BY INTUITION," says Prince Louis Albert de Broglie. He's speaking of his decision to purchase Deyrolle, the famed Parisian natural sciences store, in 2001, but really it seems true of most of his decisions. A lover of nature—and the 1831-vintage taxidermy emporium—from childhood, de Broglie saved the shop from financial ruin only to see it devastated by fire in 2008. Although 80 percent of the shop's inventory was lost, including its collections of insect specimens, scientific library, and, of course, the animals, a band of art-and-fashion-world luminaries came together to raise money for Deyrolle's restoration, and today it is as glorious as ever. De Broglie defines its mission as "inspiration, description, preservation."

Known jokingly as the "gardener prince" for his devotion to sustainable farming, de Broglie sees the shop as a valuable tool for educating people about biodiversity and ecology. Deyrolle continues to publish exquisite renditions of its original, illustrated natural science guides, and in 2007, de Broglie reintroduced the publication of a new line of the company's fabled educational charts, now dealing with subjects such as sustainable development, climate change, renewable energy sources, and endangered species.

Books have always played a role in de Broglie's life; with his brother and nephews, he is custodian of the largest private library in France. In his jewel-toned Lisbon apartment, books and taxidermy are everywhere; like Deyrolle and everything the prince does, it is a celebration of both beauty and nature. The books, unsurprisingly, have a decided bent toward natural history: eighteenth-century encyclopedias, volumes of *Astronomie Populaire,* beautifully illustrated catalogs

"THE BEAUTY
OF OBSERVATION
COSTS NOTHING."

OPPOSITE Deyrolle's famed instructional posters
line a wall of the Paris offices.

257

of flora and fauna. De Broglie says a dream of his is to reread Darwin in one of the ecosystems he designed.

As he puts it, "I always think of the fact that the root of *ecology* is *ecos*—preserving our common house. But for me, the common responsibility is because we have a common destiny." Some of this feeling of responsibility arises from a family that has devoted generations to public service. "I've been raised in a world of concern and involvement, beautiful things, books. But the beauty of observation costs nothing. People need to understand the wonder of nature."

ABOVE Taxidermy in the archives.

BELOW Deyrolle's exquisite line of books on the natural world aim to educate and inspire.

OPPOSITE, TOP LEFT Beauty—and nature—are everywhere.

OPPOSITE, TOP RIGHT The tortoise was singed in a fire that decimated Deyrolle's stock.

OPPOSITE, BOTTOM The book-filled office was once Monet's studio.

ABOVE Books on the natural world in de Broglie's Lisbon apartment.

OPPOSITE Louis Albert de Broglie in Lisbon.

"THE ROOT OF *ECOLOGY* IS *ECOS*—PRESERVING OUR COMMON HOUSE."

CUSTOM COLLECTIONS

STILL LOCATED IN THE SAME GEORGIAN TOWN HOUSE where Nancy Mitford worked as a bookseller, Heywood Hill remains a wonderful—and quintessentially British—spot where readers can browse new, used, and antiquarian books, guided by knowledgeable staff, or sign up for one of the shop's famed subscription services. However, if your needs are more specific—much more specific—they offer quite a different avenue: personalized libraries. These "library building services" can be anything; Heywood Hill has compiled collections that range from the more general (dogs; fishing; "the great American novel"; World War I; Churchill) to the esoteric ("every twentieth-century aviation memoir"; "three hundred books to read before I die"; "every escapee's memoir of the twentieth century"; "the positive story of humanity"). "It could be a shelf, it could be multiroomed," says chairman Nicky Dunne who, with his team, spends months, if not years, of research on each project and sources books from all manner of channel. "It's a quixotic venture, no question." To date, they've never been stumped by a commission. But, "dragonflies—that was challenging," he admits.

ABOVE Heywood Hill caters to all tastes, even the most specific.

THE HOUSE OF BOOKS
AND FLOWERS

ROBIN LUCAS
Isle of Wight, England

ROBIN LUCAS CAN RATTLE OFF the different categories of books in his family home on the Isle of Wight with barely a glance. "Fun books down here. There's Egyptology, alpine plants, birds." This core collection, which covers the walls of the dining room, makes up only a small part of the family's library: in total, the house holds some fourteen thousand volumes.

Lucas is an artist and designer whose illustrations are much in demand from a range of commercial and private clients. However, his talents defy easy categorization: He is also a gifted gardener and interior designer who planned the lush English country garden—and productive kitchen garden—that surrounds the 1926 home. (While taking his college finals yet.) By his own account, he is rarely without a sketchbook. Having studied biology at Oxford, Lucas has a particular interest in the natural world—one that clearly runs in the family.

Fiction is all shelved on the upper floors; the dining room–cum–library is devoted to nonfiction. Of the myriad subjects on display, nature and ornithology occupy a particularly prominent place. His parents are serious birders, and as Lucas says, "It's a pretty authoritative collection," with hundreds of volumes ranging from the Victorian to the twentieth century.

Lucas's father has experience dealing in rare books, and the bulk of these are in a sort of annex attached to the main house: a labyrinth of rickety shelves containing thousands of dusty volumes on every conceivable subject. "You can always find treasures," says Lucas, of this on-site set of open stacks.

By contrast, the rest of the house is cozy and ordered. When the family bought the home in the 1980s, they began the process of returning it to its original 1920s glory. Today it has the air of a home that has been continuously inhabited by a single family, since the interior is a warm mix of heirlooms and soft textiles, old copies of

OPPOSITE Books and heirlooms form a peaceful tableau.

OVERLEAF The shelves of books—many on birding and ornithology—
are "wonky" according to Lucas.

"YOU CAN ALWAYS
FIND TREASURES."

World of Interiors, and portraits of ancestors, well-laid fires, and late dahlias.

It was Lucas's parents who installed the dining room bookshelves. "If you look at them, they're incredibly wonky," he says. "The pine was really intended for marquetry and can't stand up to the weight of the books." As for dusting, it's a weeks-long, all-hands-on-deck affair.

Lucas loves working while surrounded by his family's books and says that as a child he always looked through them: the ornithology and natural curiosities, of course. "But I especially loved architecture books." And books on garden design clearly had an influence: Gertrude Jekyll, Gabriel Hemery. Lucas says he also loves pulling books from the shelves for inspiration—particularly of the natural variety.

Although the home contains almost an embarrassment of literary riches, Lucas admits, "I'm very keen on stalking charity shops. I love looking, at least, at design books, auction catalogs—you can often find corners of rooms that you haven't seen elsewhere."

"And, of course, proper books," he says. "Although I really love audiobooks—I'm quite dyslexic, so for me they're wonderful. I can listen to them on the train while I work, all the time. And so I 'read,' in inverted commas, a great deal. That's how I read all of Dickens, and all of Austen."

A keen cook, Lucas also has a vast collection of cookery books, "in some ways what I love most." These range from the antique—think menageries of quivering Victorian puddings—to modern British. At both the Isle of Wight home and the house he is settling into in Northumberland, he says he cooks every day.

Indeed, the dining table transformed easily between a beautiful luncheon setting and a workshop for sketching and watercolors; Lucas was completing an illustrated guidebook to Tuscany. His first book was titled, appropriately enough, *The Sketchbook of a Gentleman.*

ABOVE LEFT Robin Lucas on the Isle of Wight.

ABOVE RIGHT Lucas did a stint at *World of Interiors.*

ABOVE The family's book hoard is filled with treasure
waiting to be unearthed.

ACKNOWLEDGMENTS

This book was inspired by and created with thirty-two remarkable individuals who let us into their homes and shared their stories with us. We are so thankful *to you* for allowing us to capture your personal spaces and for all your hospitality. Each of your libraries was deeply inspiring to us, and we feel lucky to be able to share them with the world.

Sadie and Shade, I could not have asked for more incredible partners in making this book. I loved every moment of traveling the globe with you—you turned this project into an adventure that I will remember forever. I am so immensely grateful to you both for agreeing to be a part of this and for trusting my vision. I learned so much from each of you; you are both masters of your craft. It was a privilege to work with you.

Sadie, it was amazing to watch your extraordinary ability to connect with people and translate each of those connections into a story. Your devotion to this project and your ability as a storyteller *is* remarkable. Your dedication brought this book to life.

Shade, you are truly a brilliant artist. Your ability to capture the most beautiful moments—and the homes and the personalities of the owners under any condition—is astounding. I am so excited for the world to see all of your incredible images; each one is truly a piece of art.

Thank you to everyone who helped connect us with the people featured in this book. A special thank-you to my friend Lesley Blume for introducing me to Sadie, and for your support throughout. Thank you to Michelle Adams, Nicky Clendening, Chloe Malle, Alex Vadukul, and Tarajia Morrell.

A tremendous thank-you to Clarkson Potter and to Angelin Borsics, my editor. Your trust in me and your dedication to this book pushed me to create something I am very proud of. You are the dream editor, and I am so lucky to be able to work with such a professional—truly the best in your field. I cannot thank you enough for allowing me to take on these journeys and explorations.

To those working behind the scenes: thank you to Mia Johnson, whose attention to detail and thoughtfulness in design and printed layout made this the book that it is. To Kim Tyner, the production manager, for your tireless effort in proofing all of the artwork, as well as Aislinn Belton, who kept us on time and on schedule. And to production editor Joyce Wong and copyeditor Shelly Perron, for working so hard to ensure the text was perfect.

And a big thank-you to Doris Cooper and Aaron Wehner, the publishers who have been incredibly supportive throughout the entire project.

Thank you to my parents, who taught me to follow my dreams and to push myself into new territory every single day.

Lastly, I lovingly dedicate this book to my husband, Mike, and my two boys, Julian and Wolf. I could not feel luckier to be able to come home to all of you every day. Mike, your support means everything to me, and you've truly helped make my dreams come true. Julian and Wolf, it is a privilege to be your mother and to be with you as you both grow, evolve, and become beautiful humans. I hope this book inspires you to view the world with open eyes, cultivate a natural curiosity about the environment around you, and, above all else, nurture a love of books and storytelling throughout your lives.

OPPOSITE Annotated books in the home of R. O. Blechman.

270

Interior designer and founder of Haus Interior®, NINA FREUDENBERGER is the author of the bestselling design book *Surf Shack: Laid-Back Living by the Water*, which was featured in *Architectural Digest*, *Vanity Fair*, *O, The Oprah Magazine*, and *Vogue*. She lives with her husband and two boys in Los Angeles.